PUB WA

— IN —

Shropshire

THIRTY CIRCULAR WALKS
AROUND SHROPSHIRE INNS

Kate Pybus

COUNTRYSIDE BOOKS
NEWBURY, BERKSHIRE

First Published 1994
© Kate Pybus 1994

COUNTRYSIDE BOOKS
3 Catherine Road
Newbury, Berkshire

ISBN 1 85306 305 3

Designed by Mon Mohan
Cover illustration by Colin Doggett
Photographs and maps by the author

Produced through MRM Associates Ltd., Reading
Typeset by Paragon Typesetters, Queensferry, Clwyd
Printed and bound in England by Woolnough Bookbinding,
Wellingborough

Contents

Publisher's Note

We hope that you obtain considerable enjoyment from this book; great care has been taken in its preparation. However, changes of landlord and actual closures are sadly not uncommon. Likewise, although at the time of publication all routes followed public rights of way or well-established permitted paths, diversion orders can be made and permissions withdrawn.

We cannot accept responsibility for any inaccuracies, but we are anxious that all details covering both pubs and walks are kept up to date, and would therefore welcome information from readers which would be relevant to future editions.

Area map showing locations of the walks.

Introduction

Travel beyond the Midlands and a Salopian soon tires of trying to explain where exactly Shropshire lies. We smile resignedly as city-types chuckle at our invisible county. And then we return. Enough footpath to stretch from here to Omsk in Siberia and no danger of erosion by the tourist's foot, lanes so quiet that you are far more likely to meet a rabbit than a car.

But Shropshire is much more than a pretty place. It is the cradle which rocked the Industrial Revolution, the talents of Wilfred Owen, Britain's finest war poet, Mary Webb, the novelist, and Housman's 'A Shropshire Lad'. The cries of centuries of Border warfare ring through our castles and Iron Age hill forts. Each of these short walks is an opportunity to discover the county's historical riches as well as its tranquil beauty.

The threat to the traditions of the great British pub has been much talked about elsewhere. Young Salopians may never tire of complaining about our lack of clubs, cinemas and fast-food restaurants, but the lack of competition has kept our country pubs very much alive. Some of these pubs I discovered in my own misspent Shropshire youth, some are Shropshire classics, while others were found with a little help from friends. Before setting off on a walk, be sure to ask the publicans if they mind you leaving your car for a couple of hours. They will be happy to oblige as long as you observe this simple etiquette.

For most of the walks you will need a good pair of waterproof boots or shoes. You may also like to take iron rations such as nuts or chocolate and a bottle of water. The walks are accompanied by simple sketch maps, but you will get more out of them if you invest in an Ordnance Survey map. All the maps recommended are in the OS Land-ranger series. Sheets 126, 127, 137 and 138 cover all of Shropshire. They can be very useful as they indicate all the public footpaths.

Kate Pybus
spring 1994

Market Drayton
The Clive & Coffyne

When is a coffyne not a coffin? When it's a piecrust. This pub specialises in pies: pork and apple, and lamb and apricot are exciting reworkings of traditional English flavours; for the more simple piemen, there is steak pie or beef cobbler. There are also vegetarian dishes, sandwiches and home-made puddings. The *pièce de résistance*, however, has to be the Clive Pie: a little pie with a long history.

Robert Clive is known worldwide for his exploits in India. Here, in his home town, they celebrate a more private side to the man: his love of good food.

In 1768 Clive was recuperating in Pézenas, a town in south-west France. In gratitude for the kind reception, he presented the town with a pie. In Pézenas they have stayed true to Clive's original *petits pâtes* and, as a reward for their loyalty, now sell around a quarter of a million pies a year. It was not until 1990, when the Clive & Coffyne opened, that the pie, a subtle combination of lamb, dried fruit, lemon and spices, could be tasted on home shores. Crowned by Guinness as the best traditional dish in the country, the little pie has gained national acclaim.

Half-timbered and full of Clive memorabilia, the pub is open 11 am to 3.30 pm and 7 pm to 1 am Monday to Saturday, 12 noon to 3 pm

7

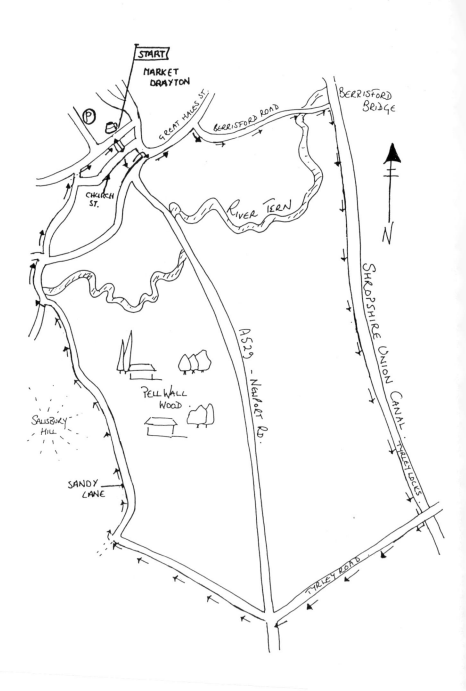

and 7 pm to 10.30 pm on Sundays. Food is only served at lunchtimes and not on Sundays at all. There are Tetley and Burton real ales, and Copperhead cider. Children and dogs are allowed only in the beer garden.
Telephone: 0630 653263.

How to get there: The Clive & Coffyne is in the centre of Market Drayton in Shropshire Street. The X64 bus service runs Shrewsbury – Market Drayton – Hanley via Newcastle-under-Lyme.

Parking: There is a small car park behind the pub, which is inaccessible on Wednesdays due to the street market. There is an alternative car park at Towers Lawn, where Frogmore Road and Cheshire Street intersect.

Length of the walk: 4½ miles. Map: OS Landranger 127 Stafford and Telford (GR 350670).

Through the stomping ground of young Robert Clive and along the most beautiful section of the Shropshire Union Canal. The entire walk can be enjoyed year-round as it is on well-surfaced tracks. Although there is a fair amount of road-walking, within ten minutes of the start point the roads become high-hedged lanes with overhanging oaks, where you are more likely to encounter a rabbit than a car. The rich agricultural land never ceases to roll, but always quietly, supporting some of the 10,000 cows whose milk goes to the giant Müller yoghurt plant in Market Drayton.

The Walk
Fortified with a packet of the town's celebrated gingerbread, turn right out of the pub car park and right again past the Clive's front entrance. Take the first left down St Mary's Street.

Ahead of you is the tower of St Mary's Church. In his boyhood, Clive climbed the tower and, straddling one of the gargoyles, waved to the townsfolk below. Legend has it that he wanted to recover a smooth pebble from the gargoyle's jaws for a game of 'ducks and drakes' in the river Tern. The gargoyle is preserved in the museum in Powis Castle.

Cross Church Street into the churchyard. Follow the path around the church. Take the short flight of steps down to your right. The building named The Old Grammar School is famed as the first of several schools to expel young Bob before he was shipped off, at the age of 17, with the East India Company to Madras. Ironically, a desk-top with the carved initials R.C. is now reverently preserved in the headteacher's study at the local school.

Follow the path past the building and down Clive Steps. On your

9

right is a paved area with benches, on the wall a small plaque recounting the life of the 'heaven-born general'. Glancing to your left before crossing over to the petrol station, there is another site of young Clive's enterprise and leadership. He led a gang of lads in a sort of protection racket. When one of the shopkeepers on this hill refused to pay the levy of sweets or pennies, Clive planned to flood his premises by damming the rainwater pouring down the gutter. When the dam broke before the plan could be carried out, Clive is said to have thrown himself bodily into the breach.

Safely over the road, go down Great Hales Street. Walk past the cottages and the church of St Thomas and St Stephens. Follow the curve of the high red-brick wall on your right and walk into Berrisford Road. On your left is the Grove School. In 1830 Grove House, which now houses the sixth form, was bought by Charles Wilson the great canal contractor and lasting friend to Thomas Telford. During the building of the nearby canal, Wilson at one time was employing more than 2,000 'navigators', or navvies as they were later called. The Wilson family lived in Grove House for over 100 years.

Cross the Tern by a little stone bridge. Ahead of you is the aqueduct, which carries the canal over both road and river. Take the sandstone steps up the right-hand side to the canal. Follow the towpath to the right.

When the Birmingham and Liverpool Junction Canal was opened in 1835, it was one of the last narrow boat canals to be completed. The threat of the railways was already apparent. The emphasis had shifted from linking one town to another, to providing the most direct link between the manufacturing centres of the West Midlands and the ports. To reduce the time taken by the journey, Telford drove his canal straight across the landscape. Ignoring the contours demanded a new technique of construction with dramatic cuttings and massive embankments. Alas, Telford's pioneering cut-and-fill technique, whereby rock from the cuttings was used to build embankments elsewhere, was rapidly copied by the railways themselves. The race was lost. The achievement remains phenomenal, especially when you think that the only tools were the picks and shovels of the navvies.

From this elevated section of the canal there are excellent views of the surrounding fields and trees: ash, larch, oak and sycamore. The bird-life includes chiff-chaffs, herons, moorhens, tree-creepers and woodpeckers.

After a few hundred yards you enter a red sandstone cutting stained with sea-green lichen. In canal jargon, cutting through the rock was known as 'rockin'. It now makes an excellent habitat for bats and kingfishers.

Before Bridge 60 is an angular lock-keeper's cottage. If this should remind you of the toll-houses on the old A5 London–Holyhead road, it's a case of Telford being economical with his designs. Go under the bridge and make a hairpin turn up to the right. The attractive wharf and cottages were built in 1837 for shipment of milk from the nearby Peatswood Estate. Earlier this century, when Cadbury's had constructed their factory along the canal at Knighton, a boatman known as 'Chocolate Charlie' collected milk and took raw materials to the Bournville factory in Birmingham.

Cross the stile and go left up the lane. After about ½ mile, cross the busy A529. Should you feel like a drink (already), the Four Alls, a 16th century pub with an intriguing sign, marks the halfway point. Follow the lane running down the side of the Four Alls until it veers to the right down a lane Sandy by name and nature.

On your left is Salisbury Hill, now part of the golf course. In 1489, during the Wars of the Roses, the Earl of Salisbury and his 5,000-strong army camped here. Two and a half miles east they met the Yorkists at Blore Heath and 'the Hemp Mill Stream ran red with blood'.

To the right, at the dip in the lane, you will see a low red-brick house and walled garden, surrounded by stately conifers. This was the gardeners' house and kitchen garden of Pell Wall, the last domestic building of the architect Sir John Soane. The outlying buildings and parkland are now a far better testimony to the great architect than the house, which has been derelict since a fire in the early 1980s. Plans for its restoration are, however, afoot.

Continue down the track, passing a massive gnarled sweet chestnut on your left and eventually out to a road. Turn right towards the sound of rushing water. This stretch of the river is so clear it is common to see trout basking on the river bed. Bishop Heber, of *From Greenland's Icy Mountains* fame, could have composed *The Terne* whilst sitting on Walkmill Bridge:

I love to tread the little paths, the rush banks between,
Where Terne in dozy silence creeps through the meadows green.
I love to mark the speckled trout beneath the sunbeams lie,
And skimming past, on filmy wing, the danger courting fly.

At the junction cross the road; two roads lead straight ahead. Take the one to the right: Kilnbank. It is a fairly steep climb through the sandstone cutting, but now you are only minutes away from a pint and a pie. Emerge from Kilnbank on to the Shrewsbury road. A little way to your left is Fairytale Gingerbread. The bakery makes a huge variety of novelty gingerbreads. Turn right down the Shrewsbury road into the town centre. The Clive & Coffyne is on your left.

Hampton Loade
2
The Lion Inn

The Lion Inn has a long and distinguished history in the fine art of providing food and drink to the weary traveller. In the early 1600s it was a cider-making house; in the 19th century, while slaking the thirst of a village toiling in the heat of its iron smelting furnace, the Lion ran a sideline in hand-made violins: today the inn specialises in a cuisine soaked in country wines, hand-blended on site for over 30 years.

The restaurant menu offers delicacies such as venison, guinea-fowl, or duck, in wines flavoured with orange, apricot, elderberry or birchbark – in all, 24 varieties. The bar menu includes simpler fare such as cottage pie, vegetarian meals, steaks and ploughman's.

The inn is Tardis-like in its proportions, with bar, lounge bar, restaurant and an attractive dining area which was formerly the stables. The décor is traditional with aged oak beams and fireplaces. There is a large range of real ales including Wood, Boddingtons and Hook Norton. Children are welcomed for bar meals at lunchtimes, and in the evening if booked into the restaurant.

Summer season opening times are Tuesday to Sunday 12 noon to 2.30 pm (3 pm Sunday), 7 pm to 11 pm (10.30 pm Sunday). From October to end of March the pub is closed weekday lunchtimes except Christmas and Easter.

Telephone: 0746 780263.

How to get there: 1 mile off the A442 between Bridgnorth and Kidderminster.

Parking: There is plenty of parking space at the Lion and an alternative car park at the ferry.

Length of the walk: 6 miles whether taking the circular route, or walking into Bridgnorth and returning by steam train. Map: OS Landranger 138 Kidderminster and Wyre Forest area (GR 748862).

A circular route from Hampton Loade via Bridgnorth by ferry, field and footplate. Beginning with a ferry ride across the Severn, the walk follows the Severn Valley, through woodland, across open fields, and past sandstone cliffs, into Bridgnorth, returning on the Severn Valley Railway, Britain's most picturesque steam railway. There is an alternative route following the river and returning to Hampton Loade on foot via the reservoir and the village of Chelmarsh. Trains run regularly in summer, but there are no trains in January and February, and they are somewhat sporadic from October to April, so it is advisable to check train times before setting out. A 24-hour talking timetable can be reached on 0299 401001. At the time of writing, an adult single from Bridgnorth to Hampton Loade was about £3.50; children travel free, when accompanied by an adult, and dogs travel anywhere for about £1.

The Walk

Walk away from the pub, down the lane and over Papermill Brook. Continue down the lane. The row of cottages on your left was built around 1800 for the employees of the iron forge. At the bottom of the lane continue straight on through the car park to the jetty.

There has been a ferry at Hampton Loade since the 17th century. When the collieries were open it was needed to transport the miners. The passengers may have changed, but the service has retained the personality of a bygone era. In summer there is often a small group waiting at the jetty, but in winter there may be only one passenger in a day. Ring the bell on the post and you will see the two sisters, who have been working the ferry since the '50s, emerge from the cottage opposite. The ferry is propelled by the current and guided by cables and a rudder. At the time of writing the trip cost 20p and 5p for dogs; the last ferry is at 8.15 pm.

Alighting from the ferry, go right following the river path through a campsite and under a modern and rather playful bridge carrying two pipes across the river. The tranquillity of this stretch of the river is broken only by the sound of the trains steaming between Hampton Loade and Bridgnorth.

If you are taking the circular route back to Hampton Loade, cross Mor Brook, and then go left following the brook to emerge on a lane.

13

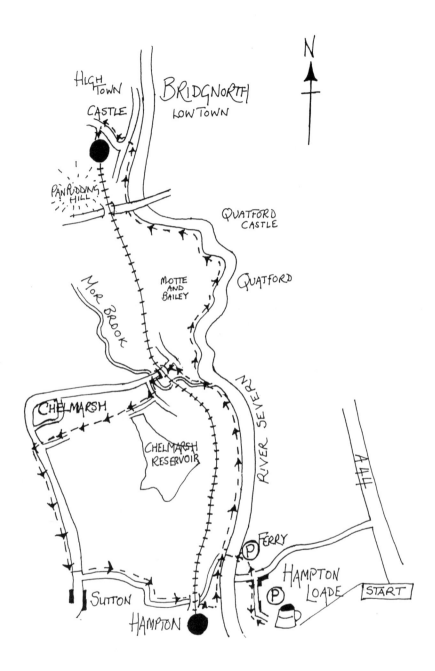

Go left along the lane, which dives under the railway bridge. Take the first narrow lane on your left. At the farm buildings, turn right, off the lane. Follow the path across the end of Chelmarsh Reservoir. The path becomes an ancient lane, deeply worn to its sandstone bed. Continue along the lane until you come out beside the ashlar stone church of St Peter. Built in 1345, this church is one of Shropshire's finest examples of medieval architecture. Go left, along the lane. Take the first left to Hampton, and return to the Lion Inn by ferry.

For the round trip to Bridgnorth, continue following the river path. On your left, behind the sewage works, you can see the flattened surfaces of a very large motte and bailey. On the opposite bank, riverside holiday homes sit like little cricket pavilions beneath the sandstone cliffs of Quatford.

As you approach the modern bridge, which carries the bypass over the Severn, Bridgnorth comes into view. The town is divided by the river: High Town and Low Town are connected by Britain's only inland cliff railway. The little green mound on your left is Panpudding Hill, once the site of a medieval castle. On July 15th, 1645 Parliamentarian troops assembled on the hill and bombarded Bridgnorth with cannonfire. Cromwell oversaw the battle personally, but the attack failed. Finally, in April the following year, the Roundheads mined the castle and the Royalists surrendered. The castle was destroyed except for the tower which leans at 17°, a greater angle than the Tower of Pisa.

Follow the river under the bypass, toward town, until you see a small flight of steps leading to the main road. Emerging on the road opposite the sandstone cliffs, go left. Walk along the pavement for about five minutes until you see a sign pointing left to the railway station.

The Severn Valley Railway, formed in 1853, ran from Shrewsbury to Hartlebury. The passenger service stopped in 1963 although trains continued to carry freight to Buildwas Power Station until 1965. In 1966, the Severn Valley Railway Society agreed to buy the line between Bridgnorth and Hampton Loade for £25,000. Although the County Council originally opposed the plans, the line reopened on 23rd May 1970.

Alighting at the tiny station in Hampton, go left out of the station, to a way-marked gate on your right. Cross the gate and walk across the fields toward the river, keeping to the left-hand boundary. Cross the footbridge and when you reach the river path, go left. You soon arrive at the ferry jetty, where you can make the return trip to the Lion Inn.

③ Ironbridge
The Tontine Hotel

The ironmasters who built Ironbridge had an eye for business. From the day work began tourists were attracted to the great iron structure like magnets. The ironmasters capitalised on this trade by building a hotel, and being a hard-headed breed, raised the capital with a tontine, a form of financial Russian roulette, invented by the Italian banker Lorenzo Tonti. Investors would receive an annual interest, increasing as each subscriber dies, until the last remaining subscriber took the whole income.

The Tontine Hotel stands in a commanding position at the end of the bridge. Its flavour is Victorian, from the foyer tiled by Maw & Co of nearby Jackfield, through to the cast-iron fireplaces in the bar.

There is a wide choice of hot and cold bar food and a children's menu, which can be enjoyed in the bar, where the last man to be hanged in Shropshire was apprehended, or on the front patio with its privileged view of the 'stupendous iron arch'. Those on an ironmasters' day out might prefer to dine à la carte or table d'hote in the restaurant. Real ales include Banks's Bitter and Mild, and Bass. Food is served all week from 12 noon to 3 pm, 6 pm (7 pm on Sunday) to 9 pm.

Telephone: 0952 432127.

How to get there: If you are approaching from the north you should cross the river at Jackfield Free Bridge (from the town centre you take the B4373, direction Bridgnorth). Almost as soon as you cross the river, take the minor road to the right in the middle of an outrageous hairpin bend. Carry on until you come to the car park just south of the Iron Bridge. From the south there is a turning off the B4375 at Broseley, or stay on the B4373 until the same hairpin before you reach the Severn and the Iron Bridge.

Parking: Parking on the town side of the river is short term and limited. A large car park has been created on the site of the old railway station just over the Iron Bridge. The bridge is for pedestrians only.

Length of the walk: 3 miles. Map: OS Landranger 127 Stafford and Telford (GR 672034).

With so much of interest in the towns of Ironbridge and Coalbrookdale, it is easy to overlook the contrast with the south side of the river. Following the tracks of the Severn Valley Railway, alas dismantled before the visitor boom could have saved it, the walk climbs through Benthall Woods, described by Arthur Young 200 years ago, as 'one immense sweep of hanging woods . . . the finest effect imaginable ', and offers views of Buildwas Power Station.

Reaching the top you are rewarded by the 16th century elegance of Benthall Hall and the curious cast-iron gravestones of the church.

The Walk

Walk out of the Tontine Hotel straight across the Iron Bridge. As well as linking industry on the two banks of the river, the bridge was built as an advertisement for the skills of the Coalbrookdale ironmasters. From the moment work commenced in 1777, it was a remarkable success. Tourists came from all over the world to see this elegant iron structure and to witness the narrow gorge aflame with furnaces and smoking lime-kilns.

By the 20th century the town's prosperity had vanished. It was described by one observer as a 'squalid town . . . covered in slag and refuse'. Yesterday's squalor is today's romance and Ironbridge is now a World Heritage Site. In the last 20 years, with a growing interest in the roots of our industrial society, disused factories, derelict warehouses and ruined cottages have been restored..

After crossing the bridge turn immediately right down the first of two tracks. Keep to the path running along the river bank until after several hundred yards you see a broad track leading up to the left, under a disused railway bridge. Go left under the railway bridge. Climb up to the right and then follow a broad track. This is the disused

17

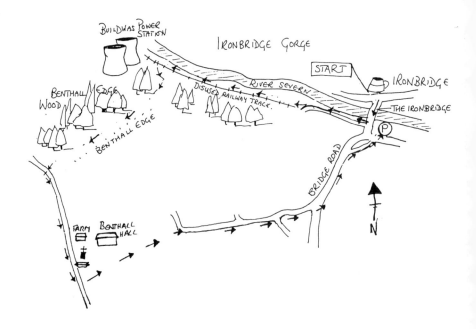

railway track. The railway, built in 1863, ran north from Coalport to join the line from Wellington to Stafford. Through the trees you can glimpse the graceful Albert Edward Bridge carrying the railway over the Severn to the limestone quarries at Much Wenlock. It was constructed in 1863 by the Coalbrookdale company at their Horsehay works, one of the last cast-iron bridges. Today it carries the coal to the power station.

As you continue along the track you will hear rushing water. This is the condensed steam running down the inside of the cooling towers at Buildwas Power Station. Continue along the track until you come face to face with 375 ft of rosy-coloured brick. Buildwas Power Station won an architectural award in 1973 for its concordance with the environment.

The disused railway track comes to a dead end at a fence. To your left is a path leading up through the woodland. The path leads uphill, to the left, for a short distance to a bench where the path forks. Take the left-hand fork which climbs steeply through Benthall Woods up a flight of steps. Long before the Industrial Revolution, Benthall Woods was an important coalfield. The monks of Benthall were among the first miners. The wood is riddled with pack-horse tracks, primitive railways and mine shafts.

At the top of the steps you will see Broseley down in the valley to your left. Hairpin to your right for a short distance, and then take a second flight of steps on your left. The steps climb to the top of Benthall Edge. Go right along the edge. The route follows a trail marked by spots of blue paint on the trees. Bear right at two forks in the path, keeping to the trail of blue spots. The trail leads through the woodland along the ridge top.

Follow the path as it dips and then climbs out of the wood, emerging on a gravel track with a stile and gateway on the left way-marked as part of the Shropshire Way. Go over the stile and follow the farm track straight ahead. On your left you will pass a beautifully preserved farmyard, with a half-timber and brick barn. Just after the farmyard on the left is Benthall church.

The church replaced an earlier building destroyed in the Civil War. There are several cast-iron tomb-stones in the churchyard. The fervour for cast iron in this region spread even to the funeral business.

From the churchyard you can see Benthall Hall. The Hall was built in the 16th century and played an important role in the Civil War, largely because of its key position in relation to the Severn. Until 1645 it was held by the Royalists, but Cromwell's men took Benthall in the same month that Shrewsbury fell. In the late 19th century George Maw, of ceramic tile fame, lived here. He planted almost every known variety of crocus in the gardens. The Hall is still renowned for its spring and autumn displays and can be visited from April to September on Wednesday, Sunday and bank holiday afternoons.

From the churchyard walk back on to the lane. Just beyond the church on the left is a way-marked spring-gate. Go through the gate and follow a distinct track across the field. From here there is a lovely view of Benthall Hall, its garden separated from the field by a ha-ha. Go through a kissing-gate in the far left-hand corner of the field. Continue down the left-hand field boundaries until you reach a farm track. Go right down the track and continue as it descends steeply and becomes a lane. At the fork bear left into Spout Lane. The name comes from a spring hidden in the woods on your left.

At the main road turn left. In the 18th century this road carried the burden of traffic created by the growing iron industry. Bricks, coal, iron ore and limestone passed this way before crossing the Severn by ferry.

The woodland to your right was the site of furnaces, smithies and a mill, and Maw's first tileworks, which moved to Coalport in 1883. A concrete footpath leads off the road to the right and back into the car park.

④ Stottesdon
The Fighting Cocks

Earlier this century a jury of 17 cider drinkers sat around the bar in the Fighting Cocks and witnessed The Fabulous Nipper Cooke down 40 pints of cider in a single sitting. Arthur Cooke, odd job man, poacher and reprobate, known to all as Nipper, died about 50 years ago, but locals still fondly regale you with his antics.

This 17th century pub is a delightful mix of locals, hikers, friendly service and home-cooked pub food. High-class snacks like whitebait, home-made pâté and toast, soup and sandwiches are served any time during opening hours. The restaurant menu includes classic pub food such as gammon, scampi, steak, goulash, steak and kidney pie and plaice. The pub has been ingeniously restored, incorporating an oak winch from the outhouses mounted on the high oak beams, an open fire and pews.

Real ales include Marstons, and Banks's Bitter and Mild, and there is draught cider. Children are welcome. Opening hours are 12 noon to 2.30 pm, 7 pm to 11 pm (except Sunday evening and Monday lunchtimes barring bank holidays).

Telephone: 0746 32270.

How to get there: Stottesdon is off the B4363 Bridgnorth – Cleobury Mortimer road. Turn off at Billingsley to Chorley and Stottesdon.

Parking: There is a large car park behind the pub and some parking in the village.

Length of the walk: 3 miles. Map: OS Landranger 138 Kidderminster and Wyre Forest area (GR 672828).

Stottesdon stands on a hillside between the Severn and the Clee Hills. The church is famed for its Saxon font, said by some to be the finest in the kingdom. Behind the church is the Fox and Hounds, a secular watering hole which brews its own beers. This gentle walk takes you to Stottesdon Bridge, along the banks of the Rea brook and the river Rea. The return journey traverses open countryside, offering wide vistas across the agricultural land to the Clee Hills.

The Walk
Turn left out of the Fighting Cocks. On the right-hand side of the road is Stottesdon church. St Peter's is of Saxon origin. The west doorway in the tower dates back to the Norman Conquest. The celebrated font has a great round bowl carved with strange beasts like centaurs and birds and bordered with a band of scrolls reminiscent of Celtic motifs.

A little further into the village, running up the left-hand side of a row of modern houses, and before you reach the Fox and Hounds, is a grassy track leading up to the left. Follow the sunken track until it enters a copse. Just inside the copse on the left are two stiles leading into the left-hand field. Cross the stiles and walk down the right-hand field boundary, following the line of the sunken track on your right.

Go through a metal farm gate in the far right-hand corner, on to a track. There is a farm on your left. Turn right, walking up the farm track to the lane. When you reach the lane go left. The lane veers right and then runs downhill to the river Rea. Cross the bridge at the bottom of the lane. Immediately after the bridge, just before the road bends sharply right, cross the stile on the left.

The path heads left cutting across the spur of the Rea. The stile is just to the left of the red-brick house. Just to the right of this house is Hardwick Forge. This was one of the charcoal forges which were scattered around Shropshire. Cross the stile and walk straight across this short field to a stile in the opposite boundary. Cross the stile and follow the river bank to the next boundary. Cross the stile to Stottesdon Bridge. This sturdy stone bridge is an ancient monument, believed to be Roman. Just over the bridge, to your left, ran the Cleobury Mortimer and Ditton Priors Light Railway. The line was opened in the summer of 1908, and linked the quarries on top of

21

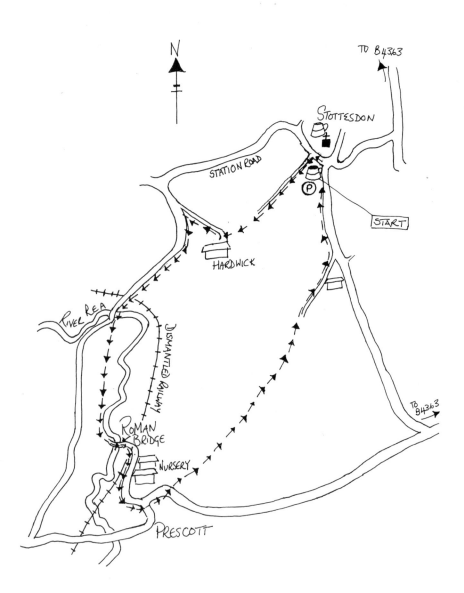

Brown Clee to the GWR line at Cleobury Mortimer. As something of an afterthought passenger carriages were added, and primitive earth platforms were erected in the villages. In the '30s both the quarry traffic and the passenger service ceased. All that remained was an agricultural freight service, carrying sugar beet, animal feed, seed, milk, beer and flour. Once a week a train carried the cattle to Kidderminster market. In the Second World War the line enjoyed a short renaissance, when it was adopted by the Admiralty. The wagons carried shells and torpedoes from an ammunition depot at Ditton Priors. The line was finally closed in the '60s.

Cross the bridge and follow the grassy track as it veers to the right. It climbs up through a farmyard and past a nursery and coffee shop on your left. Continue climbing the track past a house and some barns on to the lane. To your right is the village of Prescott. In the 18th century there was a charcoal forge in the village. In 1750 it had an annual output of 100 tons of charcoal. Turn left along the lane. After a few yards, where the road veers right, you will see a way-marked stile on your left.

Cross the stile into a wide open field. Walk down the right-hand field boundary and cross the stile in the far right-hand corner. Cross the second field diagonally to a stile in the top left-hand corner. Cross the stile into a very small field. Cut across the corner of this field to a stile opposite. Go over this stile and walk down the left-hand boundary of a long field. Pass through a gateway to a farm track. Follow the track past a pool to a stile beside another farm gate. Keep to the track as it dips down toward a stream. Cross the stream via a stone bridge and climb up the left-hand side of the field. Then continuing in a straight line, follow a line of oaks up the centre of the field to a gateway. Cross the stile next to the gate, onto the road. Turn left up the lane. The Fighting Cocks is on your left.

Cleobury Mortimer
The Old Lion

The Old Lion at Cleobury Mortimer has re-defined the term home cooking. In this delightful former coaching inn you have the wherewithal to cook your own meal because the house speciality is 'stone cookery'. The raw ingredients, a choice of poultry, meat and fish, are brought to your table with your personal hot stone. The rest is up to you. Each stone is served with salad, jacket potatoes or chips. You can also try your hand at a fondue, and order one of half a dozen more traditional starters.

The bar is homely, with a large inglenook fireplace, settles, sofas, oak beams, an oak bar with hops hanging from the ceiling and a pet parrot. The intimate restaurant seats 20. It has an open fire, a Welsh dresser with a large collection of china, and its fair share of oak beams.

Real ales are Banks's Bitter and Mild, and Bass. Children are welcome. Opening hours are 12 noon to 2 pm, 6 pm to 11 pm. Bar snacks are served from 12 noon to 2 pm and the restaurant is open from 7.30 pm to 9 pm.

Telephone: 0299 270085.

How to get there: Cleobury Mortimer is in the south-east of the county on the A4117 7 miles west of Bewdley or 10 miles east of Ludlow. Coming from the north, Cleobury Mortimer is 10 miles south of Bridgnorth on the B4363. The Old Lion is on the main street, just east of the town centre. There are regular bus services from Bewdley, Ludlow and Tenbury Wells.

Parking: There is limited parking outside the pub, but several public car parks behind the High Street.

Length of the walk: 3 miles. Map: OS Landranger 138 Kidderminster and Wyre Forest area (GR 677760).

The route leaves Cleobury Mortimer and follows an ancient pathway down to the river Rea. It follows the river before climbing up through the hanging gardens of Mawley Hall, a red-brick stately home high on the river bank. Taking in the orchards, kitchen gardens and magnificent trees of the gardens, the route takes you back over the river via an enchanting ford. After a short walk along a lane, you may make your way across the fields toward the twisting steeple of Cleobury Mortimer's famous church.

The Walk

Leave the Old Lion and walk right along the main road to Barker's Lane leading down to your left. Walk down Barker's Lane, known locally as Egg Lane. The lane crossing Egg Lane was the main road to Worcester and Kidderminster until Telford built a new road over the river Rea in 1790. The funeral procession of Prince Arthur, Henry VIII's son and heir, passed this way. The young prince's body was carried from Ludlow Castle to Worcester, accompanied by 120 torches.

Continue straight on. The brook is officially called Burrel Brook, but it is referred to locally as Pudding Brook. At the bottom of the lane is a bridleway running straight ahead between two hedges. Follow the bridleway round a red-brick house and continue as the track becomes more overgrown. In autumn the hedgerows are loaded with hips and elderberries. The path leads to a stile. Go over the stile and follow a grassy track down toward the river Rea. The house ahead of you was once a mill. Go over the stile to the right of the gate into the house. Go through the gate opposite into the farmyard. There is a waymarked footpath to your right.

Follow the footpath right along the river bank. Go over a stile and follow the path away from the river to higher ground. Beyond the open fields behind you is the twisted steeple of the church. Ahead you can see Mawley Hall positioned high up on the opposite bank above the multi-coloured layers of trees.

25

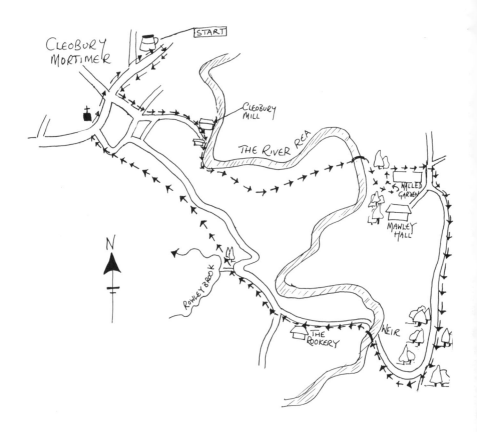

Mawley Hall was owned by the Blount family for centuries. Sir Thomas Blount was a lawyer at the court of Henry VIII. Henry sired a son by Blount's sister, Elizabeth. Desperate for an heir, Henry made him Duke of Richmond and attempted to legitimise him. The original hall was razed to the ground by Cromwell's army. This red-brick house was built in 1736 for Sir Edward Blount, the fourth Baronet.

The path runs along a ridge of earth to the left of a barbed wire fence. Follow the boundary until you meet a stile. Cross the stile and keep to the boundary as it leads you down to the Rea. Cross the river by the green footbridge, into the gardens of Mawley Hall. By the 1960s the gardens had fallen into decline. They were restored to glory by the owner, Mrs Galliers-Pratt. The path climbs for a short distance and then meets a track. Go right. Where the track forks, bear left. The path mounts slightly and hairpins round to the red-brick walls of the kitchen gardens. Follow the path along the garden walls, through an orchard, and onto a cartway. There are tracks leading left, right and straight on. Go right along the driveway leading to the hall. Just before the main gateway to the hall go left. The track leads around the hall and then heads downhill, a long majestic driveway lined with maple trees. Follow the track downhill as it dips into a woodland and curves round to the right toward the sound of rushing water.

The river crosses the track. The water is held in glassy stillness above the weir and then streams down a series of steps. Cross the river by the stone bridge and the green metal footbridge to the left of the weir. Continue along the track, climbing gently up to the horizon.

To your right are superb views of the hall. Follow the track through a gate and along a stone wall. Walk between two stables and a barn to emerge on a lane. Continue straight on up to the top of the lane and a T-junction.

Go right. The lane descends steeply. At the bottom of the hill, as the road veers violently to the right, go straight on along a muddy track. After about 10 yards a public footpath is indicated on the right. Go over this stile. The path twists up the bank of trees, and runs left to a second stile into a field. The hill ahead of you is known as 'Clavers' or 'Carvers'. It is believed a terrible battle between the Welsh and the English took place here in 1056.

The path runs down the middle of this narrow field to a gateway between an oak and an ash on the opposite boundary. Walk diagonally across the second field to another gateway. Walk along the right-hand side of the field, to the left of some farm buildings. As you climb slightly the twisting spire emerges on the horizon. Head for the spire and go through the gap in the opposite hedgerow. Keep walking in a straight line toward a stile opposite. Cross the stile onto Lion Lane. Climb the lane to emerge on the High Street opposite the church.

The famous twisted spire is due to warping of the wooden supports. The church was founded by Roger Mortimer, whose family gave their name to the town. One of the panes in the large window above the altar is dedicated to William Langland, a 14th century poet born in Cleobury Mortimer. Langland wrote *The Vision of Piers Ploughman*, a medieval poem second in importance only to the work of Chaucer.

Go right to return to the Old Lion.

6

Much Wenlock
The George and Dragon

A visit to the George and Dragon is like a visit to the Old Curiosity Shop, or to a favourite aunt who never threw anything away: from the beams hangs the largest collection of whisky water jugs in the country; cigarette cards, posters, beer trays, metal and neon advertisements cover the walls from the oak beams down to the Victorian tiled floor; propped against the walls are numerous unidentified antique objects; the telephone, cigarette machine, cash register and wireless are all museum pieces; even in the toilets adverts for Lux and Coal Tar soap battle away to sell you a flawless 1950s complexion.

Stilton and walnut pâté, pea and ham soup, casserole of beef and ale, lamb curry and pickles, home-baked ham and Cumberland sauce, chicken in Shropshire mead, or ploughman's with Shropshire Blue are just a selection from the predominantly English (or colonial) menu. There are also vegetarian meals, baked potatoes and sandwiches with a variety of unusual fillings.

In the evenings meals are served in Eve's Kitchen surrounded by pictures of Georges fighting dragons. The menu is extended with steaks and fresh fish. Real ales include Hook Norton Best Bitter, guest beers are on handpump, and there is draught cider. Tanners of Shrewsbury has chosen the wines.

Opening hours are Monday to Sunday 11 am to 2.30 pm, 6 pm (7 pm in winter) to 11 pm. Food is served 12 noon to 2 pm, 6.30 pm to 9.15 pm. The restaurant is shut on Sunday evenings and the pub closes on Mondays between Christmas and Easter. Well-behaved children are welcomed in the restaurant.
Telephone: 0952 727312.

How to get there: Much Wenlock is on the A458 between Bridgnorth and Shrewsbury. There is a bus service from Shrewsbury and Bridgnorth.

Parking: There is no parking at the pub. Much Wenlock has public car parks in Barrow Street and High Street.

Length of the walk: 3 miles. Map: OS Landranger 127 Stafford and Telford (GR 623000).

A gentle climb from the miniature market town of Much Wenlock to the wilds of Wenlock Edge: beautiful in every season, but most dramatic in winter. The walk follows well-marked paths past a striking view of the Wrekin, a disused windmill, abandoned limestone quarries and limekilns, to the haunting beauty of Wenlock Priory.

The Walk
From the George and Dragon go left up High Street. The timber-framed house on your right is called Reynald's Mansion and is 16th century. In the second block of houses on your right is Ashfield Hall, also 16th century. Charles I stayed here en route to the battle of Edgehill.
At the end of High Street turn right and then take the first left over a disused railway line. The Wellington – Wenlock – Craven Arms line, was part of the GWR empire. It ran for 100 years, between 1862 and 1962. Although the journey must have been idyllic, only 3 trains a day made the complete route, taking 15 minutes to travel 3 miles between Wenlock and Buildwas.
Continue over the bridge, and up the track opposite to the plantation. Take the right-hand path. The path meanders between the pine trees before emerging at the north-east corner of the wood, into a field. Go over the old stile into the field. Follow the right-hand boundary hedge straight uphill to Edge Wood.
When you reach Edge Wood, turn right. Looking back in the direction of Wenlock, the plump pink cooling towers of Buildwas Power Station lie to your left, and on the far right is the column-crowned Breidden Hill. In winter you can see through the trees of

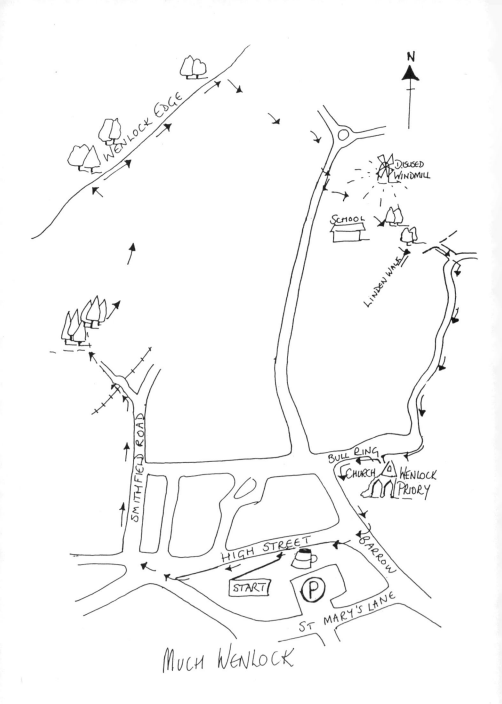

Edge Wood across the Shropshire Plain.

Walk right along the Edge. Cross two boundary lines. At a third boundary, follow the hedge round to the right. Walk back toward the town keeping to the field boundary. Behind you, looming 1,334 ft out of the undulating agricultural land, is the Wrekin. Although the Wrekin was never a volcano, it is formed of volcanic ashes and lava. It is over 600 million years old, one of the county's oldest hills.

Go over a stile and straight down the centre of a field, following a line of telegraph poles, to a gateway on to the road. Turn right down the road, until you reach a metal gate on your left. Go through the gate and walk along the well-defined path running along the base of the field. A disused windmill stands on top of the hill.

Follow the path into the wood. Up to your left are the disused limestone quarries. The path twists through the wood. Ignore the kissing-gate on the right, leading to Gaskell Recreation Ground, and continue along the path until it leads down to a sunken lane. Leading off to the right of the lane is a flight of concrete steps. Climb the steps and follow the path to a sandy lane.

The field opposite was the site of the limekilns. They were built into the hillside, taking advantage of the gradient. The kilns were charged with broken pieces of limestone and fuel from the high ground, and the burnt lime was taken out at the low front. Lime is used in agriculture, as lime mortar in building or as flux in iron smelting.

Turn right down the sandy lane. It runs along the stone wall of the priory. Wenlock Priory is the oldest known monastic foundation in Shropshire. The ruins testify to what must have been a lavish range of buildings. The infirmary and priory lodge, built around 1500, are among the finest pieces of domestic architecture of the period in England.

Continue past the priory into the Bull Ring. The tiny cottages of stone and timber framing give you the impression that you are in a village rather than a market town. Turn left out of the Bull Ring past the Holy Trinity church. Continue along Wilmore Street to the Guildhall. Built over the medieval lock-up in the 16th century. You can visit the upper room which has the original Jacobean panelling. Turn right into High Street and back to the George and Dragon.

Ditton Priors
The Howard Arms

7

The Howard Arms is a listed building about 700 years old, constructed of limestone and dhu stone, a black basalt found only on the Clee Hills. It has historical associations, not only as the former home of the Howard family, but also for playing host to Clement Attlee.

'The Village Bar' combines the warmth and tradition of an ideal country pub: dark oak bar and beams, leather armchairs and two open fires. Guest beers are on draught and Bass, Carling Black Label lager and Olde English cider are kegged. Home-cooked bar snacks are served including sandwiches, soup, Stilton quiche, and more substantial meals like beef goulash, steak and kidney pie or sausage, egg and chips.

If you prefer something a little more sophisticated, the restaurant offers dishes such as sea bass with fennel, roast duck hymeltus with walnut and herb stuffing, or pheasant Vallée d'Auge.

Well-behaved children are welcome. The pub is open 11.30 am to 2.30 pm (Sunday 3 pm), 7.30 pm to 11 pm (Sunday 10.30 pm). The restaurant is open Tuesday to Sunday 7.30 pm to 9 pm and Sunday lunchtimes. Accommodation is available.

Telephone: 074 634 200.

How to get there: Signposted off the B4364 Ludlow to Bridgnorth road, 10 miles west of Bridgnorth. The Ludlow – Bridgnorth bus service passes through Ditton Priors.

Parking: In the pub's car park.

Length of the walk: 4½ miles. Map: OS Landranger 138 Kidderminster and Wyre Forest area (GR 609892).

The summit of Brown Clee stands 1,772 ft above sea level, the highest peak in England south of the Pennines, and once the highest coalfield in Britain. In spite of a long history of mining and quarrying, the hilltop has retained an extraordinary natural beauty. The ruined buildings, the hummocks of tufty grass, and a lake occupying one of the former quarries add to the romance. The ascent is nice and gentle, through fields and along well-maintained Forestry paths. The downhill section follows the line of the Cleobury Mortimer and Ditton Priors Light Railway. The walk returns via the lanes, through the lovely village of Ditton.

The Walk
Ditton Priors lies 800 ft up Brown Clee, so you have under 300 ft left to climb. From the Howard Arms cross straight over the road and walk up the lane alongside the 13th century church. Where the lane bends right, take the tarmac road on your left. It leads down to a stile. Cross the stile into the field. Walk down the right-hand side of the hedgerow. Go over a stile in the opposite hedge, leading to a lane. Take the gravel path leading up the left-hand side of the house opposite. It crosses and recrosses the brook and emerges in a field. Walk away from the stream, crossing the field diagonally and go over the opposite field boundary. In the second field walk to a stile in the top left-hand corner. Go over the stile to the lane.

Go right for a few yards. As the lane veers sharply right, go straight on up the farm track. Pass two terraces of houses and Hall Farm, and follow the track through the farm gate into the field. The path follows the hedgerow straight up the right-hand side of this large field and through a gateway in the opposite boundary. In the next field keep the boundary on your left, cross the opposite fence by way of a rough stile made of two large rocks and a fence. Continue to climb in a straight line, up the middle of the next two fields. In the last field, head for the cottages in the top left-hand corner. The path comes out on the lane via a path running between the two cottages.

On the lane go right, up to the T-junction and then turn left. Pass the incline up Brown Clee, go over the bridge and past two farms. The lane starts to descend. On the right is a way-marked stile and a sign indicating the Forestry trail. Cross the stile. Ignoring the second stile

33

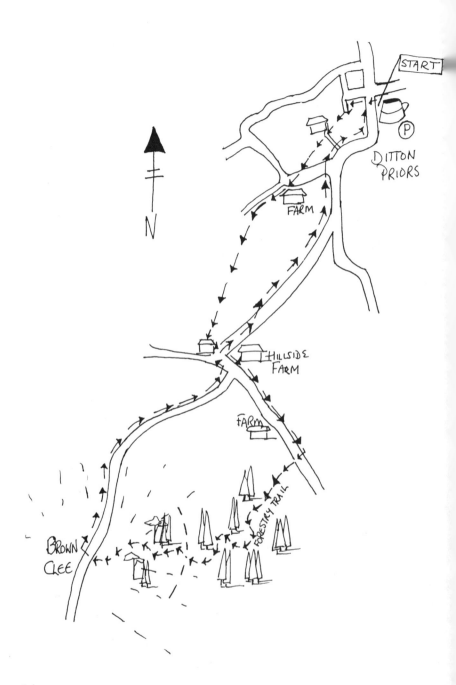

START

P

DITTON
PRIORS

FARM

HILLSIDE
FARM

FARM

FORESTRY TRAIL

BROWN
CLEE

N

34

on the left, follow the heathy track up through the bracken and gorse. The track climbs steadily, displaying a panoramic view of the surrounding plain. It then veers left, crossing a stream and running up the right-hand side of a pine wood. Keep on the path and cross a stile leading to a tarmac Forestry track.

Go left down the track until you see a stile and gateway on your right. Cross the stile and take the path leading up through mixed woodland. The path meanders uphill until it reaches yet another gateway and stile. Cross the stile on to a broad grassy track running left to right. Go over the track and follow a narrow path directly opposite. The path weaves through the coppice of Scots pine and continues up through the open moorland. As you approach the summit, the path crosses the tufty hummocks created by mines and quarries to deposit you on the well-made track leading over the hill.

This outstanding highland spot would compare favourably with any in Britain: a heather-capped peak surrounded by plains of agricultural land. The human influence on the peak is almost as impressive as the natural beauty. The old quarry building, like a hilltop fort, stands out against the skyline. Brown Clee is extraordinarily rich in valuable minerals and rocks. In the 17th, 18th and 19th centuries, the concentration was on coal and iron ore. The coal was used both domestically and to fire tobacco pipes, bricks, tiles and pottery, known as Clee Hill Ware. The iron ore went to Bridgnorth or was dispatched to furnaces in other counties. In the 20th century, coal mining declined with the expansion of dhu stone (sometimes spelt jewstone) quarrying. This black basalt is found only on the Clee Hills and is a valuable road-metal.

Transportation was the main problem for extractive industries at this height. In 1907 work began on the Cleobury Mortimer and Ditton Priors Light Railway. The single-track line was opened in July 1908. For 30 years it carried passengers and minerals. By 1934 the quarry traffic had fallen off and in 1938 it stopped taking passengers.

The only way to appreciate the skill involved in sending wagons up the hill is to walk the track. At one point the gradient is 1 in 4½. Wagons were pushed uphill by two engines, and descended guided by steel cables.

Turn right, follow the road as it curves around the top of the hill and then descends to a stile and cattle grid. Continue following the incline through the pine forest and go through the gate to the lane. On the lane turn left, and then take the first right. At the bottom of the lane go left. This takes you up through the village. Pass Reg May's, a local butcher famed for his hand-raised pork pies, and continue up the road to the Howard Arms.

⑧ **Hilltop**
The Wenlock Edge Inn

Sitting in the bar at the Wenlock Edge Inn, watching the 'saplings double' on the Edge and warming myself by the woodburner, I could not help overhearing the stream of delighted customers replete with Sunday lunch.

The sturdy limestone pub is thought to have been built to house the quarrymen and their families in the 17th century. Early this century it became The Plough – the centre of the surrounding community. Ten years ago the derelict pub was brought back to life as the Wenlock Edge Inn and is now famed for two things: the warmth of its welcome and the excellence of its home-cooked food. The menu is full of both traditional and innovative English dishes such as pork, chutney and apple pie, rich beef cobbler, porky pie, and apricot and chicken quiche. Those lamenting the demise of the great British pudding will be delighted to find it alive and well on Wenlock Edge with old favourites such as lemon pud, gooseberry cake and treacle tart.

Real ales include Hobsons, Webster's, Robinson's and Yorkshire. In summer there are three guest beers on handpump and one or two in winter. Children are welcome in the restaurant, on the front terrace or in the beer garden. Accommodation is available. Opening hours are

Tuesday to Sunday 11.30 am to 2.30 pm (3 pm Sunday), 6 pm to 11 pm.
Telephone: 074 636 403.

How to get there: Hilltop is on the B4371 Much Wenlock to Church Stretton road.

Parking: There is a car park opposite the pub.

Length of the walk: 5 miles. Map: OS Landranger 138 Kidderminster and Wyre Forest area (GR 570962).

Formed in a tropical sea 420 million years ago, Wenlock Edge, exposed to the elements and surrounded by open country, gives you a great feeling of freedom. The walk takes in the viewpoints at Ippikin's Rock and Major's Leap with their respective legends, and the mystery of Hughley's missing steeple.

The Walk
From the Wenlock Edge Inn cross the road and walk straight across the car park and through a sliding gateway. Follow the blue arrows heading straight for the Edge. Ippikin's Rock is the jutting-out limestone rock. From this exposed spot you can see the Stretton Hills lying to your left. The Edge was formed as a barrier reef 420 million years ago. The plain ahead of you was a tropical sea, probably lying somewhere south of the Equator. Ippikin was a robber knight. He lived in a cave beneath this rock with his band of followers and all their loot. Unfortunately, the huge rocky crag above the cave sheered, and trapped the robbers in the cave. According to legend, if you challenge Ippikin from this rock, he will re-emerge and toss you off the rock. This is the magic taunt (to be used with discretion):

Ippikin, Ippikin,
Keep away with your long chin!

Follow the path away from the rock, and over a stile marked 'No climbing. No hammering'. Follow the steep path down through the woodland, until it intersects with a main track.
Go left, following the blue arrows pointing to Blakeway Hollow. When the track meets another broad woodland path, go right continuing to follow the blue arrows. This was the former railway track. The Much Wenlock, Craven Arms & Coalbrookdale Railway was formed in 1860. The line ran from Much Wenlock along the foot of the Edge to meet the Shrewsbury and Hereford main line. Its principal function was to transport the limestone from the quarries further

37

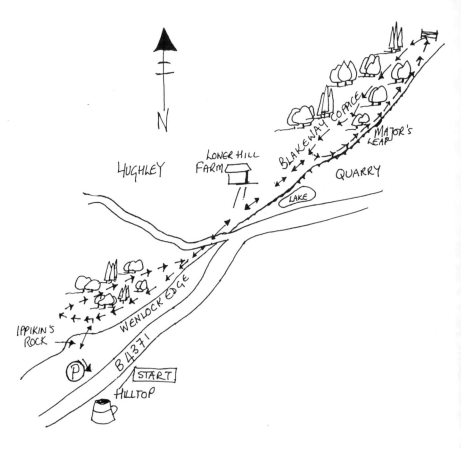

along the Edge. This idyllic route was closed in the '60s.

Continue for about a mile, until you see a clearly marked stile and gate on your left. Go over the gate and follow the path steeply downhill until you reach the road.

Half a mile to the left lies the pretty village of Hughley, immortalised by A.E. Housman:

> The vane on Hughley steeple
> Veers bright, a far-known sign,
> And there lie Hughley people,
> And there lie friends of mine.
> 'A Shropshire Lad'

If you want to go and look at the church you will not be the only visitor unable to spot the 'far-known sign'. There has never been a steeple on Hughley church, but every poet is allowed a little licence, and the 13th century church is worth seeing in its own right, having a Jacobean screen of some renown.

If you do not wish to take the detour to Hughley, go straight across the road, and walk down the wide track opposite. Do not go on to Lower Hill Farm, but continue to follow the blue arrows to Blakeway Hollow, taking the path which forks off to the right. Follow the track until you see a signpost to Major's Leap on the right.

Scramble up the steep, and sometimes muddy, bridleway to the top of the Edge. The limestone quarry below you is still very active. The white cliffs of the quarry and Corvedale beyond are a magnificent sight. If you walk a little way to your right you can see how one of the quarries has filled with water to form a cloudy aquamarine reservoir. Otherwise, walk left along the Edge.

Opposite a very old quarry is the point now designated as Major's Leap. This crag, like Ippikin's Rock, shows the exposed limestone reef, known by the quarrymen as 'ballstone'. The viewpoint is named after Major Smallman of Wilderhope Manor. During the Civil War he was riding along the Edge, with a crucial dispatch for the Royalists in Shrewsbury. To avoid capture by Parliamentarians in close pursuit, the Major rode his horse over the Edge. Major and message survived, but the horse was not so lucky.

Continue along the Edge and follow the path into a field. Walk down the left-hand side of the field for a short distance, until it emerges beside a farm gateway.

A little way down the road to your right is The Grange, the childhood home of Mary Webb, the Shropshire novelist. It seems quite likely that she took her inspiration for the melodramatic finale of *Gone to Earth* from Major Smallman's leap. Hazel, the heroine, and her fox cub plunge to their deaths over the edge of a quarry.

Doing a U-turn, go through the gate following the track back through Blakeway Hollow. Retrace the out-going route to the road and climb back up the steep track. Cross the stile onto the old railway line and take the path opposite leading uphill to the right. After about ½ mile a green arrow indicates the path back up to Ippikin's Rock. Clamber up the path and retrace your steps to the pub.

Frodesley
The Swan Inn

Sitting in the peaceful lounge bar of the Swan Inn, military manoeuvres, foreign invasion and road-works are not the first things to spring to mind. Yet the Swan Inn lies on Watling Street, the Roman equivalent of one of Hitler's autobahns, which played a vital role in the Roman conquest of Wales and the Marches. The bar and lounge bar look out on a well-preserved section of the road, running straight as a Roman nose from Wroxeter to Leintwardine.

Although they do not serve food, you are welcome to bring your own sandwiches to eat in the pub or the beer garden. Built in the 1830s, the Swan, like so many pubs in the 19th and early 20th centuries, could not survive on beer alone, and doubled as a blacksmith's and village shop. Today the village pub is again struggling for survival, and the Swan is the only remaining pub in the district. It is closed at lunchtimes, except on Sundays, but will open for larger groups of walkers. There is draught Bass and Worthington Best and kegged cider.

Opening hours are evenings, 7 pm to 11 pm, and Sunday lunchtime 12 noon to 3 pm.

Telephone: 0694 73120.

How to get there: Frodesley is 8 miles south-east of Shrewsbury. Take the A49 and turn off to Longnor. Then follow the signs to Acton Burnell. A bus service from Shrewsbury to Longnor stops in the village.

Parking: There is a car park behind the Swan.

Length of the walk: 5 miles. Map: OS Landranger 126 Shrewsbury and surrounding area (GR 514013).

The walk takes you to Pitchford Hall, the finest black and white building in Shropshire. It follows the course of Watling Street, built by the Roman army 2,000 years ago, to Acton Burnell Castle, the setting for the first meeting of the House of Commons. The route returns across the fields to Frodesley. The entire walk is on the flat, walking in a basin with the Stretton Hills to the south and the Wrekin to the north.

The Walk
Coming out of the Swan Inn, turn right down the road until you reach the crossroads, with its floral display and bus shelter. Go left in the direction of Condover. To your left you can see Caer Caradoc with its distinctive, slightly twisted summit. Continue down the lane for about a mile. The lane runs downhill. At the bottom take the bridleway on your right.

The bridleway climbs slightly, and then twists across the plain. Ahead you can see the Wrekin and, half-hidden beneath the horizon, the steaming towers of Buildwas Power Station. When you reach Stockbatch Farm, go through the gate, past the farm buildings on your right, and through another farm gate directly opposite.

Follow the field boundary down into a copse. The bridleway crosses a stream and follows the hedgerow. The path leads to a farm gate. Go through the gate, and follow the track into Pitchford.

When you emerge in the village, go left for a couple of hundred yards to the sandstone lodge. If you lean over the gate you can see Pitchford Hall, a half-timbered manor house with a charming rustic simplicity. The house was built by Adam Otley, a Shrewsbury wool merchant, in the 1560s. Among its more unusual features are star shaped chimneys and a timber-framed summer house set in the branches of a tree.

Walk back through the village, past the sandstone cottages to an entirely different kind of black and white building. The corrugated-iron Village Hall has been painted matt black with white cricket-pavilion-like porches and sheet metal chimney pots like witches' hats.

Continue down the lane, out of the village, and round the S-bend.

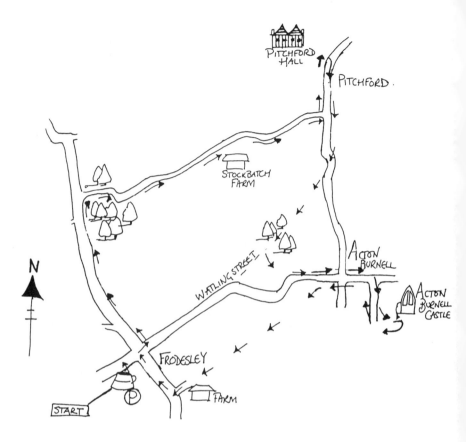

Opposite an oak tree, where the road veers left, take the grassy track leading straight on. This is a section of Watling Street. The road was probably built by the Roman army in the first century AD. Typical of a Roman road, it runs down the middle of the valley, following a straight course toward Caer Caradoc and the Stretton Hills.

As the track narrows you will come to a fork. Go left towards the sound of running water. Cross the brook by the wooden footbridge. Follow the fence on your left until you reach the metalled track. The track leads across the fields, with views of both the Wrekin and Caer Caradoc, to the lane just outside Acton Burnell.

Walk into the village, past the village shop to the crossroads. Continue straight over the crossroads. Walk down the road until you see a sign pointing right to the castle. Follow the road round to the right. On your left is the finest 13th century church in the county. The churchyard is equally impressive. The towering red trunks of the yews line up either side of the lych-gate, and amid the luscious grass of the churchyard stands a wooden crucifix.

Continue to follow the path round to a gate on your left. Go through the gate to the sandstone ruin of Acton Burnell Castle. Robert Burnell was Lord Chancellor in the reign of King Edward I. He built this fortified house in the late 13th century. If you look just beyond the field boundary on your right, you can see a stone wall, half covered in ivy. The crumbling barn wall is one of Shropshire's unsung treasures: the birthplace of democracy. In the autumn of 1283, when King Edward was fighting back a Welsh rebellion, a parliament was summoned to Shrewsbury. The parliament adjourned here to Acton Burnell. The Lords sat in the castle and the first meeting of 'the House of Commons' was held in the barn.

The main business of this first democratic parliament was to decide the fate of Daffyd ap Gruffyd, who had led the Welsh rebellion. It was elected that he should be tied to a horse's tail and dragged through Shrewsbury. Then his heart and intestines should be burnt, his body quartered and displayed throughout the realm, and his head pitted upon a lance and put on display at the Tower.

Retrace your steps back into the village. Go back over the crossroads. Where the pavement ends, on the left-hand side, there are two stiles leading into a field. Go over the stiles. Cross the first field diagonally, to a gateway on the opposite boundary. In the second field the gateway is in the right-hand corner. Walk down the right-hand side of the third field until you reach a stile and footbridge on the right-hand boundary. Go over the stile and footbridge and cross the field to a gateway just left of the oak tree.

Cross two more fields, heading toward the farm ahead of you. Walk down the farm track, with the barns on your left. Go through the white gate onto the lane. Turn right. Walk back through the pretty village of Frodesley to the Swan Inn.

10 Uffington
The Corbet Arms Hotel

The Corbet Arms stands out against the horizon with all the dignity befitting the former home of one of Shropshire's most famous families.

Following the Norman Conquest, up until the 14th century, the Corbets of Caus dominated the central Shropshire Marches. From the spacious bar or lounge bar of The Corbet it is not hard to imagine why their descendants settled on this spot. To the south, beyond the bowling green, the pub commands a view of the Severn, Shrewsbury and the Stretton Hills. The view to the north is of the distinctive ridge of Haughmond Hill.

At lunchtimes there is an ample range of traditional pub food, including duck, when available, a highly recommended steak and kidney pie, a variety of vegetarian dishes, sandwiches and baked potatoes. Booking for Sunday lunch is advisable. The evening menu is a little more formal with a good range of puds. There is Davenports real ale and Bulmer's ciders are on draught. Children are welcome in the lounge bar.

Opening hours are Monday to Sunday 12 noon to 2.30 pm, 7 pm to

11 pm (10.30 pm Sunday). Food is served 12 noon to 2 pm, 7 pm to 9.30 pm (9 pm Sunday) but no food is served on Mondays. Telephone: 0743 709232.

How to get there: Uffington is 3 miles outside Shrewsbury, off the B5062 Shrewsbury to Newport road. The Shrewsbury–Newport bus stops just outside the village.

Parking: There is a large car park behind the pub.

Length of the walk: 5 miles. Map: OS Landranger 126 Shrewsbury and surrounding area (GR 528138).

In the footsteps of the most celebrated First World War poet, those of an Augustinian monk, and a Roman legionary; along the ridge of Haughmond Hill, through deciduous woodland and across open fields toward the distant blue-tinged hills: a walk varied in both historical interest and topography.

The Walk

From the car park cross the road and over the stile directly opposite. Walk up the left-hand side of the field through a gate and over a footbridge. Follow the path between two telegraph poles and cross the stile in the centre of the opposite boundary. The route leads to a colossal electricity pylon. Bear right, walking through its powerful legs. The path passes through deciduous woodland. Head right at the fork until you reach a track running along the foot of Haughmond Hill.

Go right. Keep to the path as it climbs through the woods and wild flowers until you reach the track leading along the crest of the hill. Make a hairpin turn to the left. Continuing along the ridge, at the T-junction go left, and again left where the track forks.

This bare outcrop of rock, marked by the isolated Scots pines, is the summit. Beneath the woods ahead of you are the earthworks of an Iron Age fort. Before you lies another prehistoric sight: a panorama of the Shropshire and Welsh Hills. To the far left is the long ridge of Wenlock Edge, and beside it the Long Mynd and Stretton Hills. The shadow on the horizon to the right of the Long Mynd is the Stiperstones. Looking straight ahead to Wales you can see the Breiddens and Long Mountain. To the right, beyond Shrewsbury, is Nesscliffe and the Hopton Hills, and to the far right, distinguished by the spire of Clive church, is Grinshill.

Turning away from the view, take the track leading up to the quarry gate, and then follow the path to the left around the quarry fence. After a few hundred yards the path descends quite steeply, through the woodland to join the track skirting the base of the hill. Go right

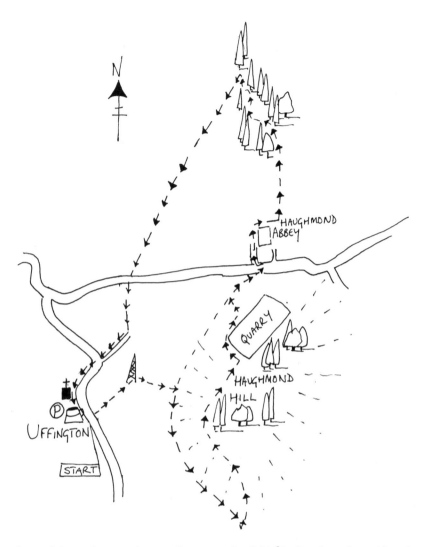

along this track, crossing a stile on to the B5062. On the other side of the road are two tracks. Take the left-hand track down to Haughmond Abbey.

When, in the 11th century, a small and austere religious community first came to Haughmond it was a comparatively wild and isolated location. Ironically, a community which had been established to counter monastic wealth soon attracted large sums from those attempting to ensure the salvation of their souls. Thus, in the 12th

46

century, Haughmond gained the status of an abbey.

Cross the stile to the immediate left of the abbey. Although now a ruin, there is still evidence of its former wealth. Opposite the entrance the magnificent late medieval bay window indicates the site of the abbot's private rooms. The vast arched window, flanked by turrets, looks on to the abbot's hall, in which guests would have been entertained. Follow the path up along the side of the abbey, past the cloisters, and then cross a stile and go left, continuing to walk around the perimeter fence.

The path intersects a well-made track. Go left, along a rocky ridge and into a fresh-smelling pine forest. Walk through the forest until you emerge at the intersection of two fields, with stiles both to the left and to the right. Across the field to the right, the clump of trees on the horizon is Ebury Wood, the site of a Roman camp.

Cross the stile to your left, heading down the left-hand side of the field, back towards Uffington. This last section of the walk opens out into wide fields, on every horizon are hills, and above, the immense Shropshire sky.

Continue down the left-hand field boundaries until you reach the road. Cross the road to a stile directly opposite. Go over the stile and follow the footpath down the right-hand side of the field. At the far corner cross the old footbridge into the left-hand field. Walk down the left-hand side of this field until the path becomes a farm track leading into the village.

At the road, go left. Among the regular congregation of Uffington church were the young Wilfred Owen and his family. The family lived in Monkmoor Road on the outskirts of Shrewsbury. One evening, as Wilfred and his brother Harold were returning from church across a field of buttercups, Wilfred remarked that Harold's boots had become 'blessed with gold' – the pollen of the buttercups. This image was not forgotten, for it reappeared in his war poem 'Spring Offensive':

> the buttercups
> Had blessed with gold their slow boots coming.

Later in the poem these same cups wait to catch the blood of the soldiers:

> earth set sudden cups
> In thousands for their blood.

No doubt these hills around Uffington would have entered Owen's mind as he fought on the flat fields of northern France.

Continue through the village to the Corbet Arms.

Grinshill
The Elephant and Castle

11

This 18th century hostelry lies in the village of Grinshill, looking up to Corbet Wood. The hotel was part of the Corbet estate and their emblem, the raven, is carved into the porch, at one time the entrance to the bar. The bar has a cosy traditional décor with a log fire, chairs and tables made from barrels, and its quota of beams and brasses. The stables and coach-house have been converted into the Grinshill Lounge, a spacious restaurant.

The Elephant and Castle is a popular haunt with devotees of classic pub food. Gammon and pineapple, chicken, duckling, steak, kidney and Guinness pie, plaice and rainbow trout are all on offer, as well as vegetarian dishes, sandwiches and for those with a hearty quarryman's appetite there is a 12 oz T-bone, or a Grinshill Quarries mixed grill. Bass ales are on draught. Children are welcome.

Open Monday to Saturday 11 am to 3 pm. Sunday 12 noon to 2 pm. Monday to Thursday 6.30 pm to 10.30 pm, Friday to Saturday 6.30 pm to 11 pm, Sunday 7 pm to 10.30 pm.

Telephone: 093 928 410/564.

How to get there: Grinshill is off the A49, 9 miles north of Shrewsbury and 4 miles south of Wem.

Parking: There is a car park at the Elephant and Castle.

Length of the walk: 2 miles. Map: OS Landranger 126 Shrewsbury and surrounding area (GR 521235).

Sandstone from Grinshill quarries has provided the stone for the Roman town of Viroconium, the doorway to 10 Downing Street and Liverpool's Anglican Cathedral. The walk takes you to the most spectacular disused quarries and along the hilltop to a panorama of the Shropshire plain. Coming off the hill, you arrive in Clive, the village which gave its name to Clive of India's ancestors. The architecture in the village displays all the varying hues of Grinshill stone, and is a conservation area. The return route follows an ancient sandstone track along the flank of the hill to the pub.

The Walk
Go left out of the pub and then take the first right up Gooseberry Lane. When you reach the sandstone village hall on your right go right, following a sunken lane running along the foot of the hill. Continue along the track ignoring a steep section of the Shropshire Way leading up to your left. At the first fork, bear right, keeping to the base of the hill. Bear left at the second fork. The deeply sunken path leads uphill. At the top there are paths leading both left and right.

A trail has recently been created through the quarries. Bear right, and you should pass a number 5 carved into a short wooden post on your left. Continue until you see a path leading to your left. Walk down this path to the rock-face. The rock varies from salmon pink to red, from grey to green. These colour variations are due to the presence of zinc, copper and lead. The soft, dark red rock at the bottom of the quarry is known as Wilmslow Sandstone. Above, the buff coloured stone is Grinshill White Sandstone, a very high quality building stone. The quarries are known as Bridge Quarries, because the stone was used to build the bridges in Shrewsbury. The keystone of the English Bridge weighed 10½ tons and took 12 shire horses to deliver.

In the right-hand corner you can look over a little stone wall into a vast square quarry. It has been disused since 1835. You can see the square holes in the rock where beams were wedged across the corners.

Walk back to the main path and go left. Ignore any paths to the right. The path becomes deeply sunken and skirts around the edge of the car park. Follow the path around the car park to emerge on a lane with two sandstone cottages on your right. The lane forks. Straight ahead is the working quarry, which has been open since 1870. Bear left down a narrow lane.

Over the sandstone walls on your right you can see the quarries

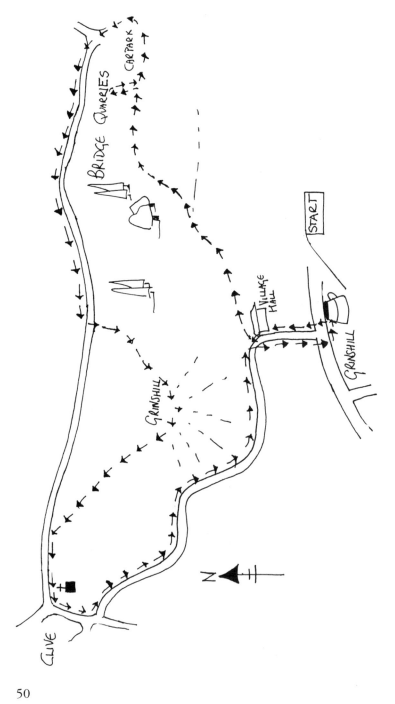

from above. Continue along the lane until you see a way-marked path on your left, leading into the wood. Go left along the path. Ignore a path off to your right. You will come to a meeting of two tracks. Continue straight on for a short distance to a point where four tracks meet around a tree. Take either of the paths off to your right.

Follow the path through the bracken, you will see a broad grassy track straight ahead. Follow the grassy track steeply uphill to the aircraft beacon. On your left is the viewpoint. You can see down to the lights of the welcoming hostelry and right across the North Shropshire plain to the Stretton Hills.

Turning away from the viewpoint go left following a rocky path through the heather. This heathland was formed between 200 and 270 million years ago when the whole area was hot desert. Bear left at the fork. The path emerges onto a well-worn sandstone lane, beside a bench.

Go left, passing Clive Primary School and several sandstone cottages on your right. This track is called The Glat, a Shropshire word meaning path or alleyway. Continue along the path as it descends steeply over great slabs of uneven rock. The Glat emerges in the village of Clive beside the church.

The church is of All Saints, the carved images of the female saints support the roof, while the males adorn the stained glass windows. In the churchyard lie the remains of William Wycherley, the Clive-born Restoration dramatist, the author of *The Country Wife*.

Until 1886 the industry in Clive was copper mining. The mine shaft is now used to house the village water supply. If you caught a whiff of wood-smoke as you came into the village it was probably coming from the Blackhursts' smoke house. In the little white building opposite The Glat, salmon, game and poultry are smoked by the traditional method, over a slow burning oak-chip fire.

Walk left down the lane and take the sandy lane on your left running along the other side of the churchyard. The track swings right and heads downhill. All along this lane, in the walls and the cottages you can see the varying hues in the sandstone. Pass the dog-rescue on your right, and follow the low red sandstone wall down to the village hall. Retrace your steps down Gooseberry Lane, and turn left to the Elephant and Castle.

Whitchurch
The Willeymoor Lock Tavern

Turn down the long drive to the Willeymoor Lock Tavern, and the pub appears to be standing in the middle of a field. Park, cross the elegant little bridges and you discover a beautifully secluded lock-side pub. This former lock-keeper's cottage was built at the turn of the 18th century, at the same time as the canal. It has been converted into a welcoming country pub taking full advantage of its location.

From the bar window narrow boats appear to rise up from nowhere as they pass through the lock. The beer garden and children's play area look out on to the water. The oak-beamed interior is decorated with a collection of toby jugs and teapots. The house speciality is the Willeymoor Grill, and the freshly battered cod is highly recommended. The menu also includes home-made lasagne, steak and kidney pie, and delightfully rich puddings like Mississippi mud pie and chocolate fudge cake. There is a children's menu and snacks such as baked potatoes and sandwiches. Theakston Real Ale, two guest beers and Tanner's wines are offered. Opening hours in summer are 12 noon to 3 pm, 6 pm to 11 pm, and in winter 12 noon to 2.30 pm, 6.30 pm to 11 pm. Food is served from 12 noon to 2 pm.

Telephone: 0948 663274.

How to get there: The Willeymoor Lock Tavern is signposted off the A49, 3 miles from Whitchurch.

Parking: There is a large pub car park. Inconsiderate walkers, in the past, have caused aggravation by parking without patronising the pub and without asking permission. Non-patrons are warned there is a £10 fine. Alternative parking can be found on the A49.

Length of the walk: 3½ miles. Map: OS Landranger 117 Chester, Wrexham and surrounding area (GR 530460).

This short and easy to navigate canal walk, would make a perfect evening stroll. The outward journey follows the canal towpath through the heart of cheese-producing country to Grindley Brook. It passes the attractive array of canal-side cottages and takes you up to Grindley Brook Locks. After retracing your steps a little way along the canal the route returns to the pub following a short section of 'The Sandstone Trail'.

The Walk
Come out of the Tavern and go right along the canal towpath. Notice the moorings along the canal bank. Work on the Ellesmere Canal began in 1793. Thomas Telford was appointed 'General Agent, Surveyor, Engineer, Architect and Overlooker of the Canal and Clerk to the Committee'. This section between Llangollen and the junction at Nantwich is now known as the Llangollen Canal, and is a very popular stretch for leisure cruising.

Pass Povey's Lock. Between Povey's Lock and Grindley Brook the canal forms the boundary between Cheshire and Shropshire. The area's most celebrated product, Cheshire cheese, is no respecter of boundaries. On both sides of the canal are the cows and pastures which produce this famous cheese. Shropshire proudly produces the prize-winning Appleby's Hawkstone Abbey Farm Cheshire cheese sold in Harrods.

The low-lying valley to your right is called the Land of Canaan, after the land between the Mediterranean and Jordan given to the Israelites. Up to your left, on the hill you can see Hinton Hall, an ominous-looking red-brick building shrouded by the trees. Continue along the towpath to Jackson's Bridge. These bridges are known as accommodation bridges. The agricultural land on either side of the canal was probably owned by one farm. Simple bridges like this connected a farmer's land which had been divided by the canal.

As you walk toward the railway embankment, the towpath is bordered by tall pampas grass. And again the moorings can be seen on the canal path leading to the bridge. The bridge carries the now dismantled Cambrian Railway at an angle over the canal. The blue bricks spiral under the arch to accommodate the skew. Pass under the bridge, and continue along the canalside past the pretty canalside cottages at Grindley Brook to Bridge 28. If you climb to the road at this point there is a mid-point pub, The Horse and Jockey. Otherwise continue along the towpath under the bridge to Grindley Locks.

On the right-hand side of the canal you can see a dairy. On the left-hand canal bank there is a large warehouse with heavy lifting equipment and a tiny red-brick hut next to the road, presumably a weighbridge. The canal rises 40 ft at this point. There are three well-spaced locks followed by a staircase of three chambers.

Climb up the flight of locks and follow the towpath under Bridge 29. On your left is a sign warning boat passengers to keep their heads down when passing through lift bridges. These distinctive and picturesque lift bridges are a rare sight on British waterways, but there are several on the Llangollen Canal. The nearest is about a mile down the canal, just before the spur to Whitchurch. On your right is a two-storey lock-keeper's cottage. This round fairy-tale cottage is a fine example of Telford's architecture.

Turn around and walk back along the towpath to Jackson's Bridge. Go through the bridge and cross the stile on your left. It is signposted 'Tushingham A41'. Cross the field to the first stile on the right-hand boundary. Immediately after it is a tiny wooden footbridge. Cross the stile and the bridge and walk up the left-hand hedgerow of the field through a gateway in the top left-hand corner. Walk up the left-hand boundary of the next field, climbing slightly. About halfway up the boundary is a stile and footbridge on the left. Cross them both. Cross this elongated field diagonally to a stile in the far left-hand corner. Go over the stile and turn left down the track passing a red-brick house on the right.

The track leads to a quiet lane. Go right. Take the first turning right down a steeply descending lane. On the bend, opposite a towering redwood, is the lodge of Tushingham Hall. Continue along the lane. You can see the hall in the valley on your right. At the bottom of the lane is a Y-junction. Go right following the sign to the Sandstone Trail. This 30 mile footpath begins at Grindley Brook and runs northward to Overton Hill on the Mersey. Continue past the farm equipment on your left to where the track forks. At the fork go left. The track ends in a farm gate. Go through the gate and walk down the right-hand field boundary. You can see the Willeymoor Lock Tavern across the field. Cross the little stile next to the beer garden and go left down the towpath into the pub.

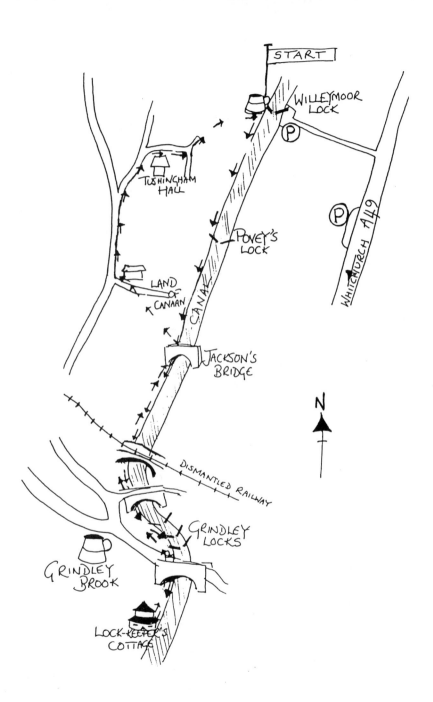

START

WILLEYMOOR
LOCK

TUSHINGHAM
HALL

POVEY'S
LOCK

LAND
OF
CANAAN

CANAL

JACKSON'S
BRIDGE

WHITCHURCH A49

N

DISMANTLED RAILWAY

GRINDLEY
LOCKS

GRINDLEY
BROOK

LOCK-KEEPER'S
COTTAGE

13 Shrewsbury
The Boathouse Inn

There were once more than 300 pubs in Shrewsbury. Overlooking the river, through the leaded windows or from the romantic terraces, it is no surprise that this 15th century pub was one that survived.

When the river was Shrewsbury's vital link to the world, the Boathouse profited from the barge traffic. During the plague of 1650, because it lies outside the Severn loop, it was a pest house, to isolate the infected. For many years a ferry brought custom from the ancient parkland opposite into the riverside garden. Boat trips still operate from the jetty.

The interior is traditional with oak settles, old bar billiards, and an open fire. Hog roast, steak and ale pie, and hot or cold baguettes are a few of the dishes on offer. Real ales include Boddingtons, Castle Eden, Theakston Old Peculier, and several guest beers, as well as draught ciders.

Opening hours are 11 am to 11 pm. Food is served 12 noon to 2 pm and in the evenings if you book. Children are welcome in the daytime.

Telephone: 0743 362965.

How to get there: Since parking is limited outside the Boathouse Inn, the walk begins from the British Rail car park in Howard Street, and arrives at the pub for a midway pause. If you are coming from Market Drayton or Whitchurch turn left immediately before the railway bridge. From all other directions, follow the one-way system first parallel to the river and then under the first part of the railway bridge (take care not to be swept round to the right). Howard Street is opposite, straight over the traffic lights.

Parking: If you use the British Rail car park in Howard Street you will need to go and buy a token at the station in the course of the walk.

Length of the walk: 2½ miles. Map: OS Landranger 126 Shrewsbury and surrounding area (GR 482123).

The history of Shrewsbury, its battles, its commercial successes, and its pattern of intimate streets and green spaces, can be told through its watery boundary. Beginning at the bottleneck of the Severn's loop, the walk circumnavigates the town centre via the ancient river-paths. Then crossing the river, it takes you through meadows to a midway pause at the Boathouse Inn. You return over the Welsh Bridge and take a short stroll through the town centre, and along the castle walls back to the car park.

The Walk

Come out of the car park onto Howard Street and go left. Walk past the main gate of the prison. Where the road swings left, go through the gate ahead, into a small garden and down the steps to the river.

Turn right along the river-path. The towpath is a legacy from the days when the Severn was a significant trade route. Men and horses would follow this towpath guiding the barges around the town to Mardol Quay. Go under the railway bridge. Behind you, above the trees, you can see Laura's Tower, the romantic gazebo added to Shrewsbury Castle by Thomas Telford. Continue along the towpath.

The narrow lane leading up to your right is St Mary's Water Lane. The 13th century arch is called Water Gate and was once a part of the town wall. On your left are the floodlights of Gay Meadow, Shrewsbury Town's ground.

Just before the English Bridge, on the opposite bank, is The Wakeman School, Wilfred Owen's former school. Also on the left, some distance from the river bank, is the truncated tower of the Abbey Church, originally founded by the Benedictines in 1083.

On your left is Coleham. The village had an iron foundry and tannery. The row of workers' cottages looks out on to the river. The remaining red-brick buildings date from the early 19th century.

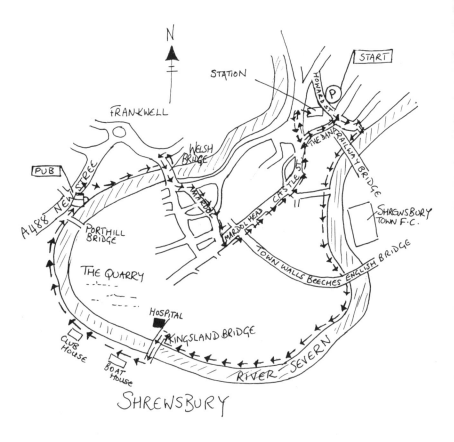

SHREWSBURY

Continue under Greyfriars Bridge and along the wide avenue of limes.

If you look up to the right, at the foot of the Roman Catholic church, you can see a remaining section of the town wall. The walls were begun by Henry III in 1226 and took about 30 years to complete.

Immediately before Kingsland Bridge turn right up the narrow lane, away from the river bank. You will emerge on the road opposite a fiery red Victorian building, complete with flying buttresses and griffins. The hospital was built in 1879 from Ruabon brick and terracotta. Go left, down the road and over the bridge. Looking through the iron arches back toward the town there is a lovely view of the pale mauve tower and green dome of St Chad's. The church is built of sandstone, not the soft red sandstone that underlies the town, but durable grey sandstone, quarried at Grinshill.

Take the steps down to the right on the opposite bank and follow the river bank past the boathouse and the boating club. Both belong to Shrewsbury School, which at one time occupied the Victorian building high up on the river bank.

This is one of the most tranquil sections of the river, flanked by green spaces and with a charming view downstream through the suspension bridge. Porthill Bridge was built by the Horticultural Society, who hold the annual flower show on the parkland on the opposite bank.

Go through the kissing-gate out of Becksfield, pass the footbridge, and into the Boathouse Inn.

Come out of the Boathouse onto the A488, go right and then right again down Water Lane, an alley leading through the horse chestnuts to the river.

Go under the Welsh Bridge and immediately afterwards take the path up to the left. Cross the bridge. Just upstream from the bridge was Shrewsbury's port. Barges exported wool, lead-ore, cheese and leather. Barges coming up from Bristol brought cloth, tobacco, spirits, wine, spices and groceries to be sold in Shropshire's markets. In the second half of the 18th century passenger wherries operated between Shrewsbury, Worcester and Gloucester.

Go slightly left down the road to the pedestrian crossing. Cross the road and go up Mardol, the road opposite. The drunken, half-timbered King's Head on your left was built in either the 15th or 16th century. On the left of the pub is an example of one of the numerous 'shuts' or passages riddling the town centre. Continue up Mardol. At the end of the street go left straight up Mardol Head, and into the pedestrian section of Pride Hill.

Thornton's, the crooked half-timbered building at number 40, is worth noting for its overhanging gable. The larger upper storeys gave the occupiers more space and protected the lower timbers from rain.

When the pedestrian section finishes, continue straight on into Castle Street.

Continue straight down the road to the station where you can buy a token for the car park. Then retrace your steps up Castle Street to a sandstone archway on your left, signposted 'The Dana'. Go left through the archway and follow the passageway along the castle wall. The castle was built by Roger de Montgomery between 1067 and 1083 on the high mound at the neck of the river. Apart from the Norman entrance, the rest was rebuilt by Edward I in the late 1200s.

To your left is a magnificent view of the railway station and the flat-iron building opposite. From this vantage point you can see the variety of architectural styles and the wrought iron decorations right on the top. Continue through the covered footbridge back onto Howard Street. Turn left to the car park.

14 Cardington
The Royal Oak

If I were dreaming of a country pub it would look like the Royal Oak. Sitting on the stone terrace amid the aroma of roses, you can contemplate the wild Shropshire hilltops, from one of its most welcoming villages. Stepping inside the tiny bar there are no fruit machines or jukeboxes to break the dream, warmth radiates from the low oak beams and a huge open fire. No wonder the Royal Oak is reputed to be the longest continuously licensed house in the country.

Sitting on one of the elm settles you can have a taste of the history, literally: Shropshire fidget pie, a mouth-watering combination of apples, onion and bacon, is an ancient local recipe. Other dishes include steak and kidney or cottage pie, soup, vegetable lasagne, sandwiches and toasties. The evening menu is extended with rump steak, chicken and gammon. The home-cooked food has earned the Royal Oak a recommendation by Egon Ronay. Wadworth 6X is on handpump, and there are Bass and keg cider.

Dogs are welcome, and children too, but in the evenings only when eating. There is bed and breakfast accommodation. Opening hours are Tuesday to Sunday 12 noon to 2.30 pm, 7 pm to 11 pm (10.30 pm Sunday).

Telephone: 0694 771266.

How to get there: Cardington is 4 miles east of Church Stretton. Turn off the B4371 at Longville, or the A49 at Leebotwood.

Parking: There is a car park opposite the Royal Oak.

Length of the walk: 5 miles. Map: OS Landranger 138 Kidderminster and Wyre Forest area (GR 505952).

Among these defiant hills Prince Caractacus made his last noble stand against the Roman invaders. The walk takes you from the enchanting village of Cardington toward the battlefield. Skirting Caer Caradoc, with its Iron Age hill fort, you climb Willstone Hill, following the ridge, before dropping down into the valley back to the pub. It is quite a strenuous walk rewarded by spectacular views throughout.

The Walk
Leaving the car park opposite the pub, turn right. Take the second road on your left, passing a small letter box, and following the wall of the churchyard. St James's contains the tomb of Chief Justice Leighton. The judge built 16th century Plaish Hall, just east of Cardington, the earliest brick-built house of its size in the country. He employed a condemned man to build the chimneys, promising him his freedom if they were the finest in Shropshire. Not surprisingly, the prisoner built beautifully ornate latticed chimneys. The judge rewarded him, so the story goes, by hanging him from his own handiwork.

At the end of the churchyard wall, cross the road and walk up the lane directly opposite. At The Old Vicarage follow the track round to the right. Ignore the track twisting round to the left and go straight on through a farm gate into a field.

Walk up the right-hand side of the field to a stile in the far right-hand corner. Cross a further five fields, keeping to the right-hand field boundary, and crossing the fences at the stiles. You will arrive at a farm gateway leading to a lane. Go through the gate, cross the lane and walk up the farm track opposite. When you meet a rusty gate, cross the stile on your left. Follow the farm track left.

This arable ridge is known as the Wilderness. Beyond it you can see two hills decorated with patches of varying greens and plum-coloured earth. Follow the track in the first field along the left-hand boundary to a stile in the far left-hand corner. Cross the stile and continue to follow the left-hand boundary downhill until you reach a large ash. Here the field widens. Walk straight ahead to a farm gate opposite. Go through the gate and on to the track.

Turn right following the track as it twists downhill. On your right the rocks on the flank of Caer Caradoc are the remains of an Iron Age

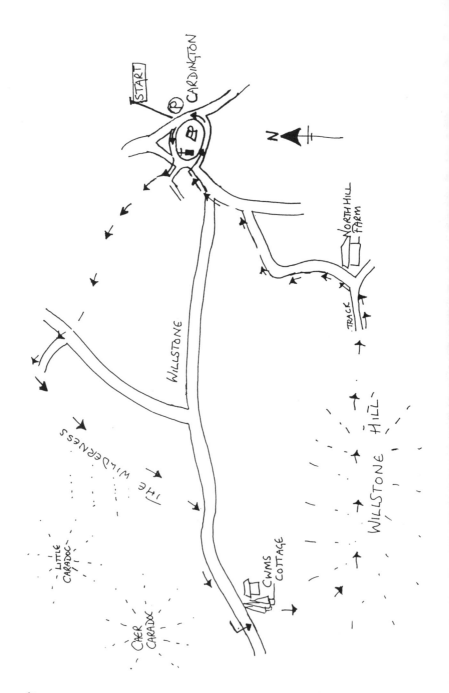

fort. Caer Caradoc is popularly believed to be the spot where Prince Caradoc (or Caractacus in its Latin form) made his last epic stand against the Romans. The Silures, a warlike tribe from South Wales, formed the bulk of Caractacus' army. He marshalled them behind the craggy stones near the summit. As the Romans scrambled up to attack they were pelted with missiles. The Roman army was, however, far better equipped than the Britons; they linked shields and advanced, breaking through the defenders' line. Many Britons were slaughtered. Caractacus escaped and hid in a cave just below the summit, on the west of the hill. He took refuge with his stepmother, but she betrayed him and he was taken in chains to Rome.

Looking up to the stunted trees lined up on the ridge of Cardington Hill, it is easy to imagine that they are foot soldiers awaiting the Roman attack.

Continue to follow the track through a farm gate. It rises and then dips through a tunnel of hawthorn and hazel. After about a mile you will see a derelict stone cottage on your left, and behind it a grove of slender Scots pines. Turn left immediately after the Scots pines. Head straight across the field toward a long brown scar in the hillside facing you. The way-marked path is in the fence opposite, slightly to the right of the brown scar, beside a large ash and a line of hawthorns.

Cross the stile and go up the path to your left. It is a steep climb through the bracken – be thankful there are no Britons hurling rocks at you. At the top of the hill, cross the stile on your left. Follow the ridge of the hill toward the rocky outcrop. Shielded from the wind, this is an excellent spot to pause and take in the view. To the southeast you can see Wenlock Edge and the Clee Hills, and to the north, the Wrekin. You may even be lucky enough to spot a kestrel hanging in the sky above the hills.

Keeping the fence on your right, continue following the ridge of Willstone Hill. The fence leads to a steeply descending field. The stile is in the bottom right-hand corner. Cross the stile, and follow a path down the left-hand side of the field. Pass a pond on your right, to a stile in the left-hand corner of the field. Cross the stile and keep to the left-hand boundary. Cross the next stile to a farm track. Go left down the track, walking downhill toward North Hill Farm. Leave the farm on your right and follow the lane steeply downhill. Pass Moor Farm on your left, and continue to the T-junction. Go left along the road into Cardington.

⑮ Ludford
The Charlton Arms

A half-timbered pub is not unusual in Ludlow, but the location of the 17th century Charlton Arms is second to none. High on the banks of the Teme, in the leafy village of Ludford, the beer garden fills with river sounds and plants cascade down toward the water. The Charlton family, whose arms grace the pub, lived across Whitcliffe Common, in Dinham House, also the 'home' of Prince Louis Bonaparte, the nephew of Napoleon, while he was under house arrest.

The spacious bar and lounge bar are oak-beamed and there is an open fire. The pub has a lively mixture of customers from globe-trotters, staying in the youth hostel across the road, to locals enjoying a game of dominoes. The menu is similarly cosmopolitan. Try crispy Camembert, vegetable samosas, or garlic and herb prawns for a starter with cottage pie, herby sausage, steaks or fisherman's platter to follow. All the food is home cooked. Sandwiches and baked potatoes are served at lunchtimes. Real ales include Bass, Worthingtons and Stones. Children are welcome. Opening hours are 12 noon to 2.30 pm, 7 pm to 11 pm. Food is served 12 noon to 2 pm, 7 pm to 9 pm. Accommodation is available.

Telephone: 0584 872813.

How to get there: Leaving Ludlow on the B4631 to Overton, the Charlton Arms is immediately on your left as you cross the river. Buses to Ludlow run from Hereford, Kidderminster, Birmingham, Shrewsbury, Bridgnorth, Tenbury Wells and Knighton.

Parking: There is limited parking at the pub, though you should ask for permission. There is an alternative car park on the route of the walk. Take the first right turn after the pub, the car park is about half a mile along the road.

Length of the walk: 5 miles. Map: OS Landranger 138 Kidderminster and Wyre Forest area (GR 513742).

The route takes you along Whitcliffe Common, overlooking the river Teme, and Ludlow and the castle. Climbing down through Mortimer Forest, with its herd of fallow deer, you emerge to a superb view of the agricultural plain. The walk then passes Oakly Park and follows a quiet lane back toward Ludlow, returning to the pub via the river path.

The Walk

Coming out of the pub, go right, walking away from the river. Take the first turn on your right. Almost immediately on your right is a path leading between the river and the road. Walk along the path, bearing left at the only fork. This is Whitcliffe Common, Ludlow's medieval grazing land.

You will emerge on the road opposite the Bowling Green Restaurant. From here you can see right over Ludlow to the Long Mynd and the Clee Hills. Ludlow Castle stands high on the river bank. It is remarkably well preserved, probably because its historical importance surpassed that of any other border castle.

During the Wars of the Roses the castle played host to Edward IV's two young sons, before they made the trip back to London which led to their deaths in the Tower. In the late 15th century it became the seat of the Council of the Marches, the body that eventually quelled the murders and maraudings which had for so long been a feature of the borders. Ludlow Castle became a royal seat, the second home of Prince Arthur and Princess Mary.

On Michaelmas night in 1634, the première of Milton's *Comus* was held here. Each summer something of the courtly splendour is revived, when it becomes the magical backdrop for an open-air theatre festival.

Go right along the road, climbing slightly. On the crest of the hill, on your left, is the gateway to North Cliff Farm. Just beyond the farm gate, is a bridleway leading up to the left. Follow the bridleway up the

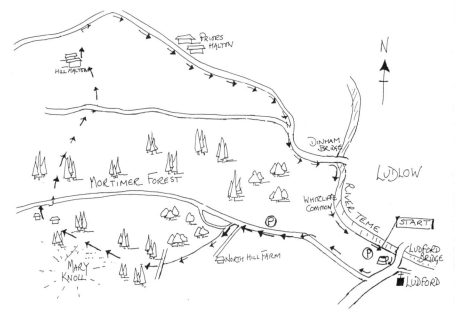

edge of Mortimer Forest. The bridleway leads uphill and becomes a
sunken lane. These tracks were formed by charcoal and timber carts,
forest industries which continued well into this century.

Mortimer Forest is famed for a herd of fallow deer which has dwelt
here since Saxon times. If you walk quietly you may catch sight of the
tufty ears and thick coats of the Mortimer Forest long-coated deer,
unique to this forest.

When you reach a tarmac Forestry Commission track you will see
a narrow track leading into the woodland. Cross the tarmac track and
go straight on into the woodland. Follow the track, ignoring the
forestry trail. To your left you will see a field and the hill known as
Mary Knoll. Continue until you come to a gateway and a stile. Cross
the stile into a field and follow a sunken path along the hedgerow,
round to the far right-hand corner. Go through the farm gate to
the lane.

Turn right along the lane. Before the lane veers right, take the path
on your left leading into a wood. The path runs downhill through the
pine forest. Cross a Forestry Commission track and continue straight
on. The path becomes very steep, still running straight downhill and
leads to a gate. Go through the gate into a field and continue walking
straight on following the line of telegraph poles. An extensive fertile
plain is spread out before you. Continue in the field to a gateway
straight ahead of you. Go through the gate and to the lane.

Turn right down the lane for a few yards, before turning left down a bridleway running between two hedges. Go through the gate and continue straight on. When you reach a half-timbered and stone house, walk to the left of it. The track goes through a gateway and toward some farm buildings. When you reach the farm go through the gate on your right, keeping the buildings to your left. You pass a ruined half-timbered cottage with leaded windows and come out on a lane.

Turn right. Follow the lane until you come to a junction. Oakly Park is on your left. The park was the hunting land for the castle 'chase'. Later it was acquired by Clive of India. Go right. Keep to the lane through Priors Halton and past the Cliff Hotel on your right. At the junction go left. As you approach Ludlow you will hear the sound of water racing over the weir. The road veers right and leads you to Dinham Bridge.

Standing facing the river, just to the right of the bridge, is a footpath running along the river bank. Follow this path, known as the Bread Walk. You will pass a quarry of Silurian limestone. This stone is particularly rich in fossils, a large collection of which can be seen in the town museum. The path gradually climbs above the river and then runs down a flight of steps to emerge on the road beside the Charlton Arms.

Pulverbatch
The White Horse

The Rob Roy Bar of this 13th century coaching inn is decked in tartan and Scottish landscapes, including a Thorburn print of a grouse, decorate the walls. It's 'Duck or Grouse' when you encounter the most hazardous of the low beams, even if it is tartan-padded. Choose from over 100 malt whiskies, and snuggle into one of the wee nooks and corners beside the inglenook fireplace.

The menu is Anglo-Scottish: Arbroath Smokies, Scottish trout, steak, chilli con carne and vegetarian platter as well as a kid's menu and snacks such as sandwiches, baked potatoes, and omelettes. Puddings include a wide choice of ice-cream sundaes, and pies such as pecan and treacle. Opening hours are 12 noon to 3 pm, 7 pm to 11 pm. Last orders for food 2 pm (1.40 pm Sunday) and 10 pm in the evenings. Telephone: 0743 718247.

How to get there: Pulverbatch is 7 miles south-west of Shrewsbury, signposted off the A488 at Pontesbury or Minsterley. A bus service runs from Shrewsbury Mondays to Saturdays.

Parking: There is a large car park at the pub.

Length of the walk: 4½ miles. Map: OS Landranger 126 Shrewsbury and surrounding area (GR 425024).

A short distance from the White Horse, high on a natural ridge, stands Castle Pulverbatch, overlooking the valley toward Wales. The motte and bailey castle was built at the time of the Conquest, as the Normans attempted to bring the ever-rebellious Marches into line. From Castle Pulverbatch, the walk takes you up to some of the wild highland scenery of Church Pulverbatch. Wilderley and Cothercott Hills provide impressive views. The return journey descends Wilderley Hill and follows the meanders of a quiet lane back into the village.

The Walk

From the White Horse turn right down the road. Where the road veers sharply right, carry straight on down Pulthey Lane. Where a track on the right meets the lane, go left into the field.

This grassy hummock is Castle Pulverbatch, known locally as 'The Knapp' from the word 'cneap', meaning hillock. The Normans arrived in Shropshire soon after 1066, where they built these motte and bailey castles to enforce control over the Marches. Castle Pulverbatch is one of the best examples. The motte is the circular mound of earth and the bailey the wall which surrounded it. A drawbridge would have run from the baileys to the motte. In the centre of the motte would have stood a wooden tower. Inside the bailey there would have been a chapel, stables and dwellings.

The castle looks over the valley toward Wales. The main medieval road from Bishop's Castle to Shrewsbury ran through the valley. During the Second World War the castle was used as a vantage point by the Home Guard, watching out for Germans invading via Welshpool. Today, the castle is a site for wild flowers and small birds to nest.

Walk back on to the lane and go left. The hedges of holly, hazel and hawthorn meet overhead to form a tunnel. Just before a large oak tree on the right, where the lane starts to climb, you will come to a way-marked footpath on your left.

Follow the path as it wends its way across the fields and down to a brook. The path is known as the Outrack. When a coffin was carried along a track, a public right of way was immediately established. The Outrack probably originated as a coffin route up to Pulthey Lane. When you reach the gate beside the brook, look down the valley. You may be able to see the traces of narrow horizontal ridges running across the field. These relics from ridge-and-furrow cultivation are probably medieval.

Cross Churton Brook, keeping to the track, and pass through another tunnel of trees. Pass the isolated habitations of the Outrack.

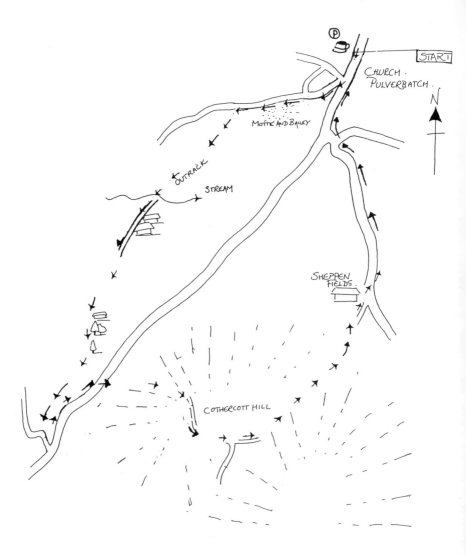

On the left the rather beautiful abandoned half-timbered building is St Paul's church.

The track becomes a path. Pass the second cottage and go through two gates. The path then leads through a pine copse and over a stile into a field. Walk down the left-hand side of the field, following Churton Brook. Cross a stile. In the second field continue following the brook for about half the length of the field. On the opposite bank of the brook is a way-marked gateway built across a tributary stream.

70

Use the stepping stones to cross the brook and go through the gate. Keep to the right-hand side of this field until you meet a stile on the right. Cross the stile into a deciduous wood. Follow the path through the wood to emerge in a marshy field. Keeping to the drier upper slopes, go right heading for a dead tree in the middle of the field.

You will meet a wide grassy track following the contours of the hill. Go right along the track. This was built as a railway running from Cothercott coal mines but was never completed. Immediately before the stone ruin of Cothercott Hill Farm take the path uphill to the left, past the ash, sycamore and horse chestnut trees.

You will come to a remote ruined stone cottage. This was built on commonland to house squatters. From here there are wonderful views of the hills ahead of you. Continue to follow the path past a stone and corrugated iron barn and into a field of thistles. Follow the line of trees up toward the horizon. Continue to follow a line of hawthorns and then keep in a straight line along a ridge of earth. The ridge leads to a stile and gateway onto a lane.

This lane would have been used by the miners working the Cothercott mines. Go left on the lane to the road. At the road go left. The road climbs up through the gorse. You will see a waymarked stile on your right. Cross the stile, and walk uphill, aiming slightly to the right. As you climb the hill you will notice it divides into two peaks. Make for a track which runs between the two peaks. This upland region bears a remarkable similarity to the Highlands of Scotland or certain areas of the Lake District.

The track was part of the former mine railway. Head for the waymarked boundary fence. Leave the line of the railway track and follow the fence down into the valley. Go over a stile. Continue walking in a straight line up through the bracken until you reach a well-defined farm track skirting the summit. Follow the farm track round to the left. The track follows the boundary fence. Cothercott Forest lies up to the right. Where the track comes to a gate, the walk joins a section of the Shropshire Way.

Go through the gate and continue straight on following a line of twisted trees. As you walk down toward the farm the views of the surrounding hills open out around you. Go through the farm gate. Walk past Sheppen Fields Farm on your left and straight down the lane. This is called Drench Lane and was the road you could see snaking down into the valley from Castle Pulverbatch. You can see the village and to the left, the rough mound of the castle.

At the junction turn left. At the Bishop's Castle – Shrewsbury road go right and climb back up into the village.

⓱ Nesscliffe
The Old Three Pigeons

Despite the pub's name, the speciality, which attracts more than a passing trade, is fish rather than game. The selection changes daily and can include blue shark, monkfish, sprats, mussels, red gurnard, Welsh herrings and many other fish you won't find at your local fishmonger. Hearty main courses include Shropshire Lass's rump, Desperate Dan's pie and duckling, as well as a vegetarian and a children's menu, and snacks. In the evenings the menu is even more extensive, and can be eaten in the restaurant.

Built in 1407 of local sandstone blocks, ship's timbers and wattle and daub, the décor remains traditional, with low beams and a huge inglenook fireplace. Beware of sitting on the seat next to the fire: it was the favourite spot of Humphrey Kynaston, the 16th century Shropshire highwayman, who terrified tradesmen travelling between Shrewsbury and Oswestry.

Real ales are Flowers Original and Boddingtons with guest beers in the summer. Opening hours are 12 noon to 3 pm, 7 pm to 11 pm (10.30 pm Sunday). Food is available 12 noon to 2.30 pm, 7 pm to 10.30 pm. Children are welcome. Booking advisable.

Telephone: 0743 81279.

How to get there: Nesscliffe is on the A5, 8 miles from Shrewsbury. Buses run hourly between Shrewsbury, Nesscliffe and Oswestry.

Parking: There is a car park at the Old Three Pigeons.

Length of the walk: 4 miles. Map: OS Landranger 126 Shrewsbury and surrounding area (GR 383192).

The walk takes you through Nesscliffe Hill Country Park to the hide-out of Sir Humphrey Kynaston, the Shropshire Robin Hood. His cave is high in the sandstone cliffs, which have been created by centuries of quarrying. The route then follows the dramatic quarry faces, past an Iron Age hill fort, and climbs through the heathland, one of the country's most threatened natural habitats, to the Cliffe. From here there are spectacular views of the surrounding hillsides. The walk returns across open fields, circumnavigating the country park, to return to the pub.

The Walk

Cross the A5 and walk a few yards down the little lane opposite, before going through a gate on your right into Nesscliffe Hill Country Park.

Follow the sunken lane round to the right, ignoring the first flight of steps on your left. Take the second flight of steps on the left up to Humphrey Kynaston's Cave. Sir Humphrey Kynaston was born into great wealth, at Myddle Castle. Despite inheriting the family fortune, his wild lifestyle soon incurred huge debts, and he was outlawed. Wild Humphrey left the castle and took up residence in this cave. He held up the merchants who travelled the high road and distributed the riches among the poor. The damp, two-roomed cave can be reached by a narrow flight of steps carved into the sandstone.

Facing the cave, walk right. The red quarry face is stained bright green with lichen, like an enormous abstract painting. You can still see the square holes where the wooden beams were held in place, the herringbone chisel marks, and the elaborately carved initials of the quarrymen dating from the 17th century.

Take the steps leading up the cliff on your left. The steps lead steeply upward to a path running along the top of the cliff. Turn left along the path. Looking down through the Scots pines to your left you can see the Old Three Pigeons nestling beside the A5. The path leads eventually to a large clearing amid magnificent oaks, birches and redwoods. Cross the clearing. At the opposite end take the middle of three paths. The path wends its way upward through rhododendrons. You will emerge at Oliver's Point, a rocky outcrop, which affords beautiful views through the Scots pines.

With your back to the view, take the path to the left of the one

73

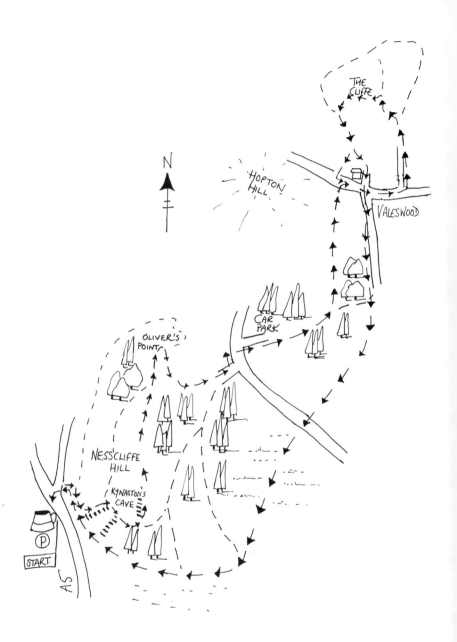

THE
CLIFFE

N

HOPTON
HILL

VALESWOOD

CAR
PARK

OLIVER'S
POINT

NESSCLIFFE
HILL

KYNASTON'S
CAVE

P

START

A5

which brought you up to the Point. The path leads downhill. Beneath the forest on your right are the earthworks of an Iron Age hill fort.

Ignore the path to your right and continue downhill. You will come out onto a track. Walk past the outhouses and an old railway carriage on your left. Continue straight on through a gateway and onto a lane. Turn left along the lane. Turn right up a track leading through the woodland to the car park.

Walk along the track past the car park on your left. Continue along the track climbing uphill, and ignoring the track to your right. At the T-junction with a tarmac lane, turn right. This attractive cluster of sandstone cottages is Valeswood village. At the telephone box carry straight on along the lane to a sunken lane on the left. Go left up the sunken lane which runs between the woodland and the fields. At the fork, bear left heading uphill to the Cliffe You are now walking through the heathland: 250 million years ago this sandy soil was a desert. This is one of few heathlands remaining in Shropshire.

When you reach the iron railings around the reservoir, walk round to the left, to the viewpoint at the summit. Looking straight ahead, west, you can see Llanymynech and the Welsh hills. Behind you to the east is the long ridge topped with lonely pines of Haughmond Hill. To the south-west is Breidden Hill crowned with Rodney's Column. To south you can make out the Stiperstones, and the Long Mynd.

Turning away from the view, with the reservoir to your left, take the small path leading through the gorse on the right. The path leads through rocks, heathers and bilberry bushes, oaks, birches and broom, so typical of heathland.

Bear right until you meet the main path leading round the base of the Cliffe. Go left. The path meets a sandy lane. Go right past a sandstone cottage on your right and on to the lane. Cross the lane and pass to the right of the telephone box, up the lane opposite. Continue along the lane, with houses and woodland on your right and open fields on your left. The lane eventually becomes a tarmac track. To the left across the fields is the village of Great Ness.

At the junction with a lane continue straight ahead through a metal gate into a field. Walk along the left-hand boundary of the field aiming for its junction with the wood ahead. Walk into the wood on the obvious downhill track. Ignore a gateway into the country park. Pass a sandstone dwelling on your right and shortly afterwards enter a gate marked 'Nesscliffe Hill Country Park'.

Follow the track around the edge of the woodland. The Breidden Hills can be seen ahead of you. The path passes the flight of steps leading up to the quarry on your right. Continue straight on. Then follow the path round to the left back to the entrance of the country park. Go through the gate and back across the A5 to the pub.

18 Ellesmere
The Black Lion

In the early 19th century, as Ellesmere flourished on canal traffic and day-trippers brought by the railway, this timber-framed pub was given a 'smart' brick frontage. A stone black lion, sprawled across the front porch, greeted farmers, canal boatmen and tourists. An ostler fed and watered the visitors' horses in the back courtyard, while they explored this newly fashionable market town.

The Black Lion is undergoing a renaissance. It has been refurbished with settles, comfy chairs, an open fire, and a snug where dogs and children are welcomed. Home-cooked bar meals served at lunchtimes include steak, mushroom and Guinness pie, roasts, freshly baked filled baguettes and spuds, as well as vegetarian dishes and a menu for the under-twelves. The evening menu includes delicacies such as fresh trout in oatmeal, Scottish mussels in white wine and garlic, and chicken tikka masala. Real ales are Marston's Bitter and Pedigree and Banks's Mild.

Opening hours are 11 am to 11 pm (closed Sunday and Monday evenings). Meals served 11 am to 3 pm, and from 6.30 pm in the evenings.

Telephone: 0691 622418.

How to get there: Arriving in Ellesmere follow the signs to the canal wharf. The Black Lion is in Scotland Street, just opposite the wharf. Bus services run from Oswestry, Shrewsbury and Whitchurch.

Parking: There is a car park behind the Black Lion. Alternative parking spaces can be found at the canal wharf.

Length of the walk: 4 miles. Map: OS Landranger 126 Shrewsbury and surrounding area (GR 400350).

For several centuries during the last Ice Age, the glaciers paused in their final retreat on a line between Oswestry and Manchester. The ice moved down from the north and melted on this line. The melt waters deposited sand and rock and filled small hollows to form meres. The greatest concentration of these lakes, nine in all, surrounds the great mound of glacial moraine, now known as Ellesmere. The walk takes you to the remarkably intact wharf on the Ellesmere Canal, and along the waterway to Blake Mere and Cole Mere. The meres are a magnet for the nature lover as well as those with a literary bent. Mary Webb, the Shropshire novelist, was inspired by Cole Mere for the mysterious setting of Precious Bane. *The mere can still capture the imagination, especially when the waters are 'troubling'. At all times the walk follows well-maintained footpaths, an easy and rewarding 4 miles.*

The Walk
Come out of the Black Lion Hotel into Scotland Street. This road does not lead to Scotland, it commemorates, the 'scot' or tax paid on land. Opposite you, on the corner of Wharf Road stands the Ellesmere Hotel, known as the Bridgewater Arms.

Cross Scotland Street and into Wharf Road and walk straight on to the wharf. Although it is no longer bustling with activity, the wharf is remarkably intact. The original crane remains and the warehouse still carries the lengthy boast: 'Shropshire Union Railways and Canal Company – General Carriers to Chester, Liverpool, Manchester, North and South Staffordshire, and North Wales.' Tucked away in the centre of Ellesmere the wharf is a peaceful memorial to the golden age of canal transport.

Walk to the right of the wharf and follow the towpath up the right hand side of the canal. When you reach the junction, cross the bridge onto the opposite towpath. Walk along the left-hand towpath. This branch of the canal goes to Hurleston and eventually on to Ellesmere Port.

The elegant round building at the meeting point of the two canals is Beech House. It was the temporary canal HQ. The curved boardroom window surveys the canal. Behind Beech House is the Canal Company workshop, still used as a dry-dock for repairing boats.

77

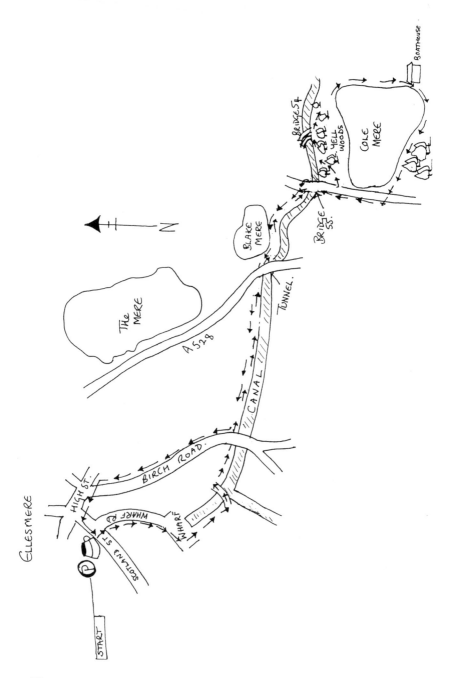

Continue to follow the towpath to the tunnel. The tunnel is 87 yards long. Canal boats were pulled through by horses walking along the towpath. The canal now passes Blake Mere. The mere is bordered by glacial moraines now covered in Scots pines, rhododendrons, oak, alder and birch. Herons, kingfishers and other water birds can be seen on the mere.

The Shropshire novelist Mary Webb used the meres' mysterious beauty as the setting for her best known novel *Precious Bane*: one night, the weaver strays from the path and is found in the morning drowned in 'Blackmere'. Prue Sarn, the heroine, dreams of curing her harelip by dressing in a white smock and stepping into the 'troubling waters' of the mere.

Continue to follow the towpath until you reach the second bridge after the tunnel, Bridge 55. The reeds in the shallow waters near the bridge are a habitat for water voles. Go under the bridge and over the stile on the left. Cross over the bridge and down the lane to a stile and gate on your left. Go through the gate into Yell Woods. As you enter the wood notice the canal raised on the embankment on your left, and a stone with the letters E.C. carved into it. This marked the boundary of the Ellesmere Canal property. These woods then passed into the hands of the Duke of Westminster, and they are now County Council property.

The track leads through the wood up to a yew tree and back onto the towpath. Follow the canal past the bridge until the path leads back down into the woodland. Walk through the wood and over a tiny stone bridge. Go through a gate to the edge of Cole Mere. In the marshy area to your left you may spot snipe, lapwing, and curlew.

The village on the left is Colemere. The church was built in 1870 on the site of an older church. Cromwell's men reputedly threw the church bell into the mere. It is said that the bell can still be heard echoing from the water's depths.

Walk along the Mere edge, over a stile and round the wire enclosure of boats. Turn right, continuing to walk round the Mere into Boathouse Wood. As you follow the woodland path to the kissing-gate look out for yellow water-lilies. Go through the gate and back onto the lane. Walk along the lane to the bridge. Go over the stile and on to the towpath.

Follow the towpath back to the last bridge before the canal junction. Leave the towpath and climb on to the bridge. Go right along Birch Road. The White Hart on your right is one of the contenders for the oldest pub in Shropshire. Continue to the end of the road. Go left along High Street and left again to the Black Lion.

⑲ Stiperstones
The Stiperstones Inn

In the heart of Shropshire's walking country, the Stiperstones Inn has maintained the down-to-earth charm of a former lead-miners' watering hole. The building is about 300 years old and, until about 25 years ago, was three in one: hostelry, farm and mine. Today it is connected to the village shop.

The lounge bar is wood-panelled with a fireplace and horse brasses. There is an intimate restaurant and a beer garden. The inn is open all day. All you need do is ring the brass bell for service. Coffee is served in the mornings, simple bar food, such as lasagne, cottage pie, chilli, sandwiches and baked potatoes, is served from lunchtimes onward. In the afternoons there are tea and cakes.

Real ales are well-kept Wood on handpump and Whitbread Best. There are picnic tables outside and children are welcome. Bed and breakfast is available. Opening hours are 11 am to 11 pm.

Telephone: 0743 791327.

How to get there: Stiperstones village is off the A488 between Shrewsbury and Bishop's Castle. Turn off the A488 at the village of Ploxgreen, in the direction of Snailbeach. Drive through Snailbeach to arrive at Stiperstones.

Parking: There is a car park behind the pub.

Length of the walk: 4 miles. Map: OS Landranger 126 Shrewsbury and surrounding area (GR 361003).

From the village of Stiperstones the route climbs through heather and whimberry, overlooking the Hope valley to arrive in Snailbeach. The road snakes through the village taking you to the lead mines, at one time the richest veins in Europe. The return route climbs up Lordshill, passes Crowsnest Dingle, and descends through the spectacular heather-clad valley of Mitton Dingle, back to the pub. An energetic walk rewarded by stunning highland scenery.

The Walk
Leave the inn and walk right down the road. Turn right passing a postbox, and heading up a rough lane. The white house on your left was one of the numerous pubs catering for the hard-drinking mining community. Continue uphill until you meet a farm gate. Go through the gate. Immediately on your left is a steep rocky path. Scramble up the path and follow the fence on your left. There are glorious views toward Long Mountain in the west. The path climbs through the whimberries and bracken and then leads up to the right, away from the fence.

Keep following the path as it snakes downhill to a white cottage. Go straight on through the two gates. The track hairpins right and becomes quite grassy. Continue downhill, over a cattle grid and out to the road. Turn right down the road into Snailbeach. This community originated with the lead and barytes mine. In the mine's heyday over 500 men were employed.

The Weigh Bridge Café, with its pretty tea-garden, stands at the point where vehicles would be weighed before they left the site. On the opposite side of the road is the metal base of a gantry crane, probably used for loading. A little further along the road is the Victorian chapel.

As the road bends around some well-kept allotments you can see corrugated-iron Nissen huts on your right: they come complete with windows and chimneys. Pass the former village shop on your right, painted green, and still sporting enamel advertisements and a Players Navy Cut cigarette machine.

Continue up the road until you come to a wide track leading up to the old lead mines on your right. Snailbeach was said to be the richest lead mine per acre in Europe. A rich vein ran east to west along this side of the hilltop. The peak years of output came in the 1850s, when 3,500 tons of ore were mined annually.

The immense spoil heaps are a striking local landmark. They remain

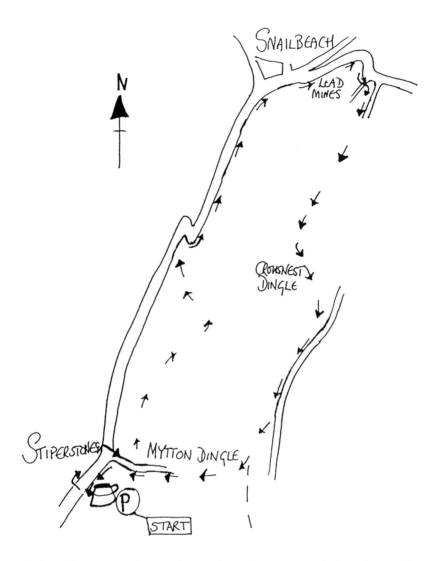

stark white, containing toxins such as lead and cadmium in which plants won't grow.

The first building on your right is the locomotive shed. The County Council, which is currently restoring the site, plans to make this the visitor centre. The Snailbeach District Railway opened in 1877 and ran on an unusually narrow and cheap gauge. In the first six years the railway was a success, carrying an average of 14,000 tons of minerals a year. Business peaked in 1918 at 26,000 tons, but by the mid-30s the

Snailbeach District Railway was a much more streamlined affair.

Driver, fitter, foreman and sole employee of the company was a man named Gatford. He continued to run the line throughout the Second World War, until, in 1947, it was leased by the County Council. The Stephens locomotives were scrapped, but the line battled on in characteristically novel fashion. A Fordson farm tractor was used to straddle the track and pull the wagons from Callow Hill to Pontesbury. This innovative arrangement continued until 1959 when the line was finally closed.

Continue up the main track until you reach a broad track running into the pine forest on your right. Follow the track past site works on your left up through the woodland to a tall hexagonal chimney. The Big Chimney was connected to the smelt mill and the Cornish engines by a long flue running underground. The flue allowed the maximum quantity of lead to be captured before the fumes were expelled.

Continue uphill following the wire fence on to the exposed heath. Carry on following the fence through the bracken to a stile leading into a field. Follow the left-hand field boundary through two fields to another stile and a notice board. Continue along the path heading uphill to Crow's Nest Dingle.

Follow the fence to the left of the Dingle, a steep-sided dell with a cottage sitting at the very bottom. Pass two corrugated-iron barns. After a fir tree the path leaves the fence for a short time, swinging right through a gate. Then keep the fence to your left until you meet a wider track leading to the right, along a stone wall.

Follow the stone wall and the line of hawthorns past a fire post. To your left, framed by the saddle of the hill, are the craggy stones of the Devil's Chair. You will meet an old track leading around the contours of the hill. Follow the track left for a short distance, heading for the valley with Stiperstones village at its mouth. A narrow path leads off to the right through the heather. Follow this path around the contours of the valley. You can see Stiperstones village down the valley. Before you reach the mouth of the valley you will meet a narrow path leading steeply off to your right. Go right, making a steep descent over the rocks through the heather.

As you approach the bottom of the valley the path follows a strip of open grassland along the valley floor. It then joins a well-made track to a farm gate. Go over the stile beside the gate and follow the lane back into the village. Go left back to the pub.

Aston on Clun
The Kangaroo Inn

Nobody knows exactly how the name Kangaroo was acquired by a Shropshire pub, but it dates from the 18th century when Captain Cook was exploring the Antipodes and returning with strange beasts to delight the rich. Ever since, this snug stone pub has been at the heart of a colourful local history. When John Marston and Mary Carter, the Romeo and Juliet of Aston on Clun, were married, Mary decreed that any travellers who visited the pub on their wedding anniversary should be bought a drink. In the 19th century Black Country horse dealers rioted here, and poachers sold their illegal gleanings behind the locked door of their den.

The pub has retained its traditional décor with heavy oak beams, stone fireplaces and pews as well as numerous pictures of kangaroos, wallabies, koalas and Ned Kelly. Classic pub food includes home-made vegetarian pie, lasagne, steaks, a range of sweets and ice-cream sundaes, snacks and sandwiches. Real ales are Bass, M&B, Highgate Mild, Welsh Brewers and Worthington. Children are welcome. The beer garden has a barbecue, picnic tables, a children's play area and a lovely show of flowers.

Opening hours are 12 noon to 3 pm, 7 pm to 11 pm. Food is served from 12 noon to 2.30 pm, and from 7 pm onwards.

Telephone: 058 87 263.

How to get there: Aston on Clun is on the B4368, between Clun and Craven Arms. The bus runs between Montgomery, Bishop's Castle, Craven Arms and Ludlow.

Parking: There is a large car park beside the Kangaroo Inn.

Length of the walk: 3 miles. Map: OS Landranger 137 Ludlow, Wenlock Edge and surrounding area (GR 392818).

Aston on Clun is a romantic place. This gentle walk takes you through the village to the Arbor Tree, a large poplar festooned with flags to celebrate a marriage that took place over 200 years ago. It follows ancient tracks through a valley compassed by hills, to arrive at the Norman church in Hopesay. The return journey cuts across Hopesay Common, skirts Hopesay Hill, then heads across the open fields back into the village.

The Walk

As you leave the car park take a look to your right at the stone round-house. There are two in the village. Go left up the road to the tree decorated with flags. This is the Arbor Tree. It is decorated annually to celebrate the marriage of Mary Carter of Sibdon Castle and Robert John Marston, heir to the Oaker estate. The couple, the Romeo and Juliet of Aston on Clun, came from rival families and the marriage brought the feud to an end. As Mary was driven to the church she was delighted to see the poplar tree blossoming in flags. She assumed the villagers had decked the tree as a celebration of her nuptials and left a legacy so that the tree could be decorated each year on her anniversary. Love is, however, notoriously blind and apparently the enchanted bride had failed to note that her wedding day was also Oak Apple Day. This day was set aside to commemorate Charles II's famous escape from the Roundheads after the Battle of Worcester. Charles had hidden in an oak tree on the Shropshire border at Boscobel. All over the country trees were bedecked with flags.

Notwithstanding, the tradition survives and on the 29th May each year a mock bride and groom are led to the Arbor Tree, and the villagers dance and revel as the flags are nailed to the trunk.

Ignore the lane running over the bridge, and a private driveway to your right. Walk down the main road until you see a farm track on your right. Walk up the track until it crosses another track at a right angle. Turn left.

The track is bordered by hedges, and climbs gently uphill. Keep to the track as it goes through a farm gate beside an oak tree, followed by a tunnel of hazels and oaks. The path leads uphill to a waymarked gate and immediately after it a stile. Go through the gate and cross the

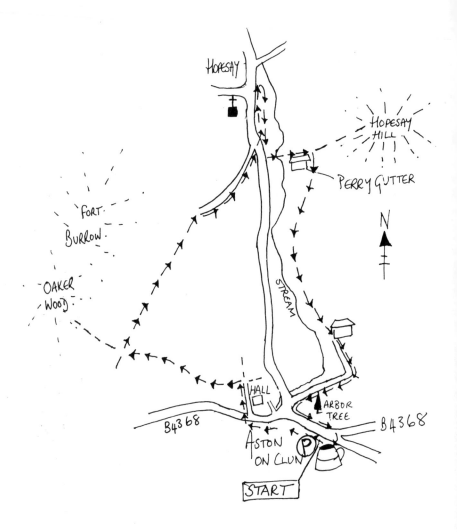

stile. There is a path leading from the left, a path leading straight uphill, and a gateway on your right. Go through the gate on your right. Follow a sunken track straight ahead. At some points it is too overgrown to walk along the track, in which case walk down the right-hand side of the field. Follow the track over a gate between two hedgerows, and into a hazel tunnel, before it emerges eventually on a lane.

On the lane go left, and left again a short distance to Hopesay Church, a 12th century truncated tower with a pyramid on top. Return to the point at which you emerged on to the lane. A little further down the lane is a small gate on the left leading into a field. Go through the gate and walk along the left-hand field boundary.

Cross the footbridge and continue to follow the boundary uphill to a wicket gate. Go through the gate and turn right. Pass a cottage on your right and go over another footbridge. Climb up to the right-hand side of the field and follow the right-hand boundary. You will meet an old grassy track. Follow the track through the fields until it emerges through a barred gate on to the lane in Aston on Clun. When you reach the lane turn right. Here is the second round-house. Go over the bridge to the Arbor Tree. Walk left through the village to return to the pub.

Bridges
The Horseshoes

This 16th century inn lies in a valley carved by ice into some of the oldest rocks in Britain. In fine weather you can sit at the picnic tables beside the East Onny river. Tucked away beneath the Long Mynd, in a tiny hamlet, accessible only by narrow lanes, this is the inn to get away from it all.

The Horseshoes was a coaching inn, lying on the road to Shrewsbury. The journey from Church Stretton, wending its way over the Long Mynd via the Burway, has to be the most spectacular in the county. After crossing the Long Mynd in a coach, something like the equivalent of a 16th century roller-coaster ride, passengers must have appreciated a jug of ale at the Horseshoes.

The Horseshoes is the sort of pub in which walkers, children, dogs and locals can all feel equally welcome. The interior is simple, with cream low-ceilinged rooms, a tiled floor and an open fire. Between 12 noon and 2.30 pm home-cooked pub food is served: vegetarian lasagne, chilli con carne, ploughman's and Shropshire Blue, or sandwiches. Real ales include Marston's Pedigree, Westons, Adnams and two or three guest beers, as well as scrumpy.

Opening hours are Tuesday to Sunday 12 noon to 2.30 pm (extension Saturday), 6 pm to 11 pm.

Telephone: 058 861 260.

How to get there: Either over the Burway from Church Stretton or off the A49 via Picklescott.

Parking: There is a car park outside the pub.

Length of the walk: 3½ miles. Map: OS Landranger 137 Ludlow, Wenlock Edge and surrounding area (GR 394965).

This gentle and easy to navigate walk follows the course of Darnford Brook along the luxuriant Darnford valley. The return route passes Wild Moor, said to be haunted by a phantom funeral procession, to arrive at Ratlinghope. This remote and timeless village was the inspiration for the village of 'Slepe' in Mary Webb's novel 'The Golden Arrow'. Finally, a short stroll along the Darnford valley sees you back at the Horseshoes.

The Walk

Go right out of the pub and then right again at the T-junction. Walk past the youth hostel. Immediately before a small stone bridge is a stile on your left. Cross the stile and follow the path alongside the brook.

The path is part of the Shropshire Way, a long-distance footpath. It follows Darnford Brook all the way to Lower Darnford Farm. You cannot miss the farm, as it is heralded by a mammoth red barn built of oxidised corrugated iron. With little navigating to do, this is an ideal opportunity for unrestrained enjoyment of this luxuriant valley. In autumn it explodes with colour: the bright green of the well-watered grass, and the reds and golds of the horse chestnuts, oaks, sweet chestnuts and sycamores. Idyllic cottages back on to the stream, in an isolation reminiscent of a bygone era. Herons, willow warblers, kingfishers and chiffchaffs all inhabit the valley.

The first settlement in the parish was on top of Ratlinghope Hill, and is called Castle Ring. After crossing the first gate you can see the outline of the ancient British camp up the side valley on your left.

Continue to follow the path through the valley to an iron gate leading on to a farm track. Go right down the farm track, past the farm buildings on your left. Cross the two footbridges and continue up the track to the lane. Go left up the peaceful lane. Follow the lane as it veers right. To your right, running parallel to this lane is a prehistoric track called the Portway. The track runs the length of the Mynd. A little further south are some burial mounds known as Robin Hood's Butts. From the mound Robin Hood fired an arrow which apparently hit the church tower in Ludlow 15 miles away.

At the cattle grid, go right into the field. Keeping the hedgerow to your left, follow the path until you reach the ruin of Marsh Farm. You are now crossing the evocatively named Wild Moor. A phantom

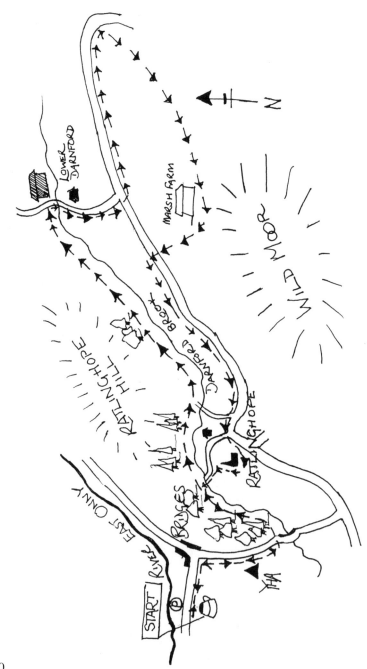

N

LOWER DARNFORD

MARSH FARM

WILD MOOR

DARNFORD BROOK

RATLINGHOPE HILL

RATLINGHOPE

BRIDGES

YHA

EAST ONNY

RIVER

START

funeral procession is said to haunt the moor. The hearse is pulled by two horses decorated with black plumes, and is accompanied by pall bearers wearing black top hats. Sightings are generally made at dusk, and it is advised to stand aside, in respectful silence, and let it pass.

Just past Marsh Farm there is a stile and gateway on your right. Cross the stile. Go straight across the field to a gate in the opposite boundary. Go through the gate on to the lane. Go left down the lane until you reach a church. This church and manor house form part of the village of Ratlinghope. The rest of the village is 2 miles away over the hill. Ratlinghope, or 'Ratchup', as it is known to the Shropshire cognoscenti, means 'the valley of the children of Rotel'. The remote and scattered community inspired Mary Webb, the Shropshire novelist, to use it as the setting for her first novel, *The Golden Arrow*. In the novel she renames it 'Slepe', perhaps because it is so quiet and has changed so little.

Go through the lych-gate into the churchyard for yet another wild Shropshire tale, a true story of a battle against the elements. The Revd Donald E. Carr ministered two parishes, Ratlinghope and Woolstaston. Each Sunday he would walk the 4 miles across the Mynd rather than walking 12 miles along the winding roads. On the night of the 29th January 1865 he set out from Ratlinghope as usual. On the plateau he was caught in a blizzard and though he had done the journey some 'two and a half thousand times', he became totally lost. Twenty-four hours later, coatless, hatless and barefoot, he crawled out into the Cardingmill valley to safety. He wrote the story of his adventure in a little book called *A Night in the Snow* and the proceeds bought a new font for Woolstaston church. The book is still on sale in Church Stretton.

Cross the stile at the far end of the churchyard to return via the gentle valley by which you came. Cross the field to the gate. Go through the gate and turn left down the track. Follow the track and cross the ford. Turn left down the path and retrace your steps to the Horseshoes.

Knighton
The Horse and Jockey

Walk into the courtyard of this 13th century coaching inn and you are greeted by a considerable choice. The bar is cosy, with an open fire and a ceiling papered in vintage sheet music. The lounge bar has a huge inglenook fireplace, large oak tables and an authentic, simple décor. The restaurant, which seats 80, was once the stabling area. Or perhaps you would prefer to sit at one of the picnic tables in the courtyard, amid the hanging baskets, potted plants and vines. In all, the Horse and Jockey can cater for over 250 people.

Despite the numbers the service remains personal. Should you fancy a dish that is not included on the substantial menu, the Horse and Jockey claims, given sufficient warning, to be able to rustle it up. The food is all home cooked and reasonably priced. Steak and kidney pudding, beef Stroganov, spare ribs, plaice and chips, monstrous chip butties, a kid's menu and vegetarian meals are all on offer. There is draught cider and Marston's Pedigree and Tetley real ales.

The pub is open all day every day except Sunday afternoons between 3 pm and 7 pm. Food is served 12 noon to 2 pm, 7 pm to 10 pm. Children are welcome.

Telephone: 0547 520062.

How to get there: Knighton straddles the Welsh border in the south-west corner of Shropshire. Take the A488 from Shrewsbury or the A4113 from Ludlow. The Horse and Jockey is in Station Road. There is a bus service from Ludlow.

Parking: The pub has a large car park.

Length of the walk: 3½ miles. Map: OS Landranger 137 Ludlow, Wenlock Edge and surrounding area (GR 285725).

Offa's Dyke is the longest archaeological monument in Britain. In 1971 the world-famous long-distance footpath was opened here in Knighton, or Tref-y-Clawdd, which means the town by the dyke. This short stroll offers you a taste of the border march. It takes you along the river Teme, before clambering up Panpunton Hill to the dyke and extensive views across Wales. The return journey leads you down through Kinsley Wood to emerge at Knighton station, where you cross the Teme back into the town.

The Walk

Come out of the Horse and Jockey, and take the first right, along a road marked 'No Entry'. This is Church Street. Pass the squat church and the half-timbered house opposite and follow the road round to the left. Turn right into Cemetery Road. The road ends at Offa's Dyke car park. Go through the gateway into the car park and follow a paved path through the picnic area. The path passes a sign welcoming you into Wales, goes through a kissing-gate and into a field.

Follow the well-worn path along the river bank. Cross a stile and a wooden footbridge over the river. Cross the Shrewsbury – Knighton – Swansea railway line. Walk across the field, aiming for the gate to the left of Panpunton Farm. Go through the gate on to a small road. Go through the left-hand gate of the two gates opposite.

The climb up Panpunton Hill is very steep, 600 ft in less than half a mile. Take a deep breath and follow the path through the trees and to the right-hand side of the grassy slope to a stile at the top. Follow Offa's Dyke path left, keeping the boundary fence on you right. Climb up to the stile at the top of Panpunton Hill. If you look over the stile you will see the dyke, running along the west of the hilltop.

Offa's dyke goes from 'sea to sea', 141 miles, a testimony to the unquestionable power, vigour and capability of its architect, the Dark Ages ruler, King Offa.

During the reign of Offa's predecessor Aethelbald, the midland kingdom of Mercia was in ascendance. When Aethelbald was murdered, civil war broke out. During the war Offa emerged as the new ruler. Offa was the first to be styled King of the English, a

93

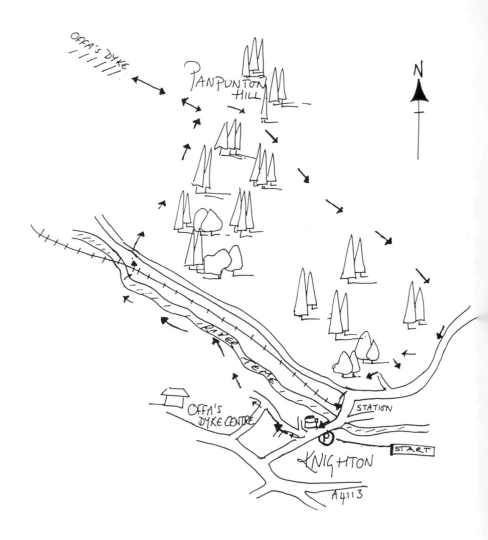

significant European figure, negotiating on a par with Charlemagne. On the home front, Offa drove back the western frontier, and after the last Welsh attack in 784, he masterminded the dyke.

Each landowner along the border would have managed the building of that section. Numerous gangs of labourers would have been recruited from western Mercia. The dyke would only have been built under a king who had outright control. A bank of earth with a ditch to the west was constructed. Wherever possible it would run along a west-facing slope on high ground to provide an optimum field of

94

vision into Wales. Here the bank may be only hedge-high, but in other respects it is a typical section of the dyke.

Looking to your right down the valley, there is a wooded knoll just beyond Knucklas. This is the site of Cnwclas Castle, or the castle on the green mound. Legend has it that King Arthur defeated the giants at this spot, and married Guinevere at the castle. You can also see Knucklas viaduct, with its fairytale towers at each end. This is where the Central Wales line crosses the valley.

Walk back down Offa's Dyke Footpath. Follow the boundary on your left, back to the stile which you met after your steep climb uphill. Climb over the stile. Head diagonally right through the oaks. Follow the boundary fence alongside Kinsley Wood for a short distance to a metal hurdle leading into the wood.

Cross the hurdle and walk straight ahead until you meet a broad Forestry track to your left. Follow the track left. It passes a field on your left and then leads steeply downhill. The path emerges from the wood, overlooking the valley. It then re-enters the wood. The path hairpins right. On a second hairpin bend, to the left, continue walking straight ahead along a path through a deciduous woodland. Follow the path to emerge onto the A488 opposite Knighton station. Cross the railway bridge back into Wales. Continue up Station Road over the river and up to the pub on your right.

Clun
23
The Sun Inn

Clungton and Clunbury,
Clungunford and Clun,
Are the the quietest places
Under the sun.

'A Shropshire Lad' A.E. Housman

While Housman's verse may still apply to the village, beneath the sign of the Sun Inn things are rarely subdued. The Sun Inn is the hub of village life and a must for all visitors. The tiny 15th century cruck building has a profusion of exposed timbers, oak beams and flagstones. You can participate in a game of cribbage, dominoes or backgammon by the open fire, or sit back in a settle or on the terrace among the potted plants.

Former restaurateurs, Keith and Bunny Strong, exercise their culinary talents on dishes such as shoulder of lamb with garlic, cashew-nut paella, wholewheat pancakes and seafood lasagne as well as classics such as ploughman's, pâtés, steaks, sandwiches and home-made puddings. Real ales are Banks's Bitter, Marston's Pedigree, Wood Special and a guest beer.

The Sun Inn is open Monday to Saturday 11 am to 3 pm, 6 pm to 11 pm, and 12 noon to 3 pm, 7 pm to 10.30 pm on Sundays. Accommodation is available. Telephone: 0588 640277.

How to get there: Clun is on the B4368, 8 miles west of Craven Arms. There is a bus service from Craven Arms to Clun.

Parking: There is no car park at the Sun Inn. Park in the river bank car park, on the opposite side of the river, just over the medieval bridge.

Length of the walk: 6 miles. Map: OS Landranger 137 Ludlow, Wenlock Edge and surrounding area (GR 300805).

Housman included Clun among 'the quietest places under the sun'. But it was not always so. The walk takes you to the picturesque Norman castle, built on the river bank to defend this border town against Welsh invasion, and climbs up through field and woodland to Bury Ditches Iron Age fort. The oval ramparts compassing the summit of Sunnyhill were until recently covered in thick pine forest. Today it is as naked as the day it was built, a magnificent example of Iron Age engineering, affording stunning views of the surrounding countryside. The return journey follows tracks and quiet lanes down the valley into Clun.

The Walk
From the car park beside the river Clun, cross the medieval saddleback bridge. Go left at the fork and up Buffalo Street to the square. On your right is the Buffalo Inn. Sir Walter Scott is believed to have written part of *The Betrothed* during his stay there. Go left up Enfield Street to the entrance to the castle on your left.

This picturesque castle, on the banks of the Clun river, is one of the finest in the Welsh Marches. Founded in the 11th century, it was the stronghold of the FitzAlans until 1549. The FitzAlans were the most prominent family in Shropshire throughout the Middle Ages. They came from Cotentin in France and were granted the lordship of Oswestry under Henry I. In 1155 William FitzAlan married Isabel de Say, who brought the Barony of Clun as her dowry.

This spectacular ruin dates from the 13th century. The Norman keep towers 80 ft above the motte, with walls 11 ft thick. A medieval garden with ponds and pavilions stood on the opposite river bank.

Come out of the castle grounds and go right along Newport Street. At the end of the street go left, following signs to the youth hostel. Pass the youth hostel on your right. Continue up the lane, until you see a track leading off the lane to the right, at a right angle. Turn down

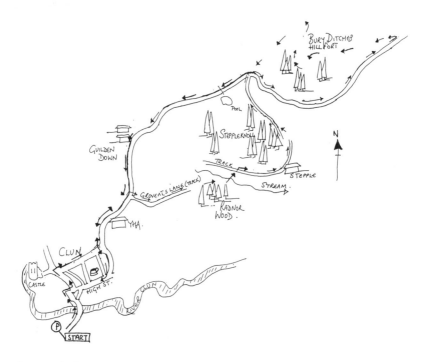

the track, known as Groveats Lane. It swings left and crosses a ford. The track parts company with the stream and climbs uphill to a stile.

Cross the stile into a field. Keep to the left-hand side of the field, and continue climbing to a gateway in the far left-hand corner. Go through the gate and follow the well-worn path down the left-hand side of two further fields. You will arrive at a gateway into Radnor Wood. Go through the gate and keep to the path running down the left-hand edge of the wood. The path drops down to a fixed gate on the left, leading out of the wood. Climb over the gate.

Ignoring the narrow lane to your left, go right into the field. Keep to the boundary alongside Radnor Wood. Go through a gate in the right-hand corner of the field. Walk diagonally across this next field. Go over a stream and climb up to the top right-hand corner, on to the farm track which runs along the top edge of the field.

Go right along the farm track, following the contours of Steppleknoll to the farm at Stepple. Go straight through the farmyard to a gate opposite. Go through the gate and keep following the muddy track around Steppleknoll. Go through a farm gate across the track. Go left, climbing up the field to the boundary fence running around the pine woods on Steppleknoll. Follow the boundary fence to your right. After a short distance you will see a waymarked stile on your left, leading into the wood. Go over the stile and turn right along the Forestry track. Follow the track as it widens and climbs to a junction with another broad Forestry track. Go right.

The track swings around Sunnyhill and offers wonderful views west into the valley and across to Clunton Hill. Follow the track until you reach the car park and picnic area where a path hairpins up to your right. Pass the plan of the Forestry Commission trails, and follow the sunken path up to the hill fort.

You enter the fort by the main entrance. High banks shelter the entrance to defend this vulnerable spot against attack. Hill forts are defended settlements, usually dating from the first millenium BC. There are two earth ramparts on the southern side where the gradient of the hill forms a strong natural defence, and four on the north. There are over 50 hill forts in Shropshire. Most of them occupy the uplands of the south and west, taking advantage of the wide views and steep slopes as a natural defence.

Climb up to the trig point. The observation point is marked with an impressive array of landmarks, including the Bronze Age axe factory at Lan Fawr, the stone circle at Mitchell's Fold and Offa's Dyke. Nearer to home, just to the north, you can see the town of Bishop's Castle. About a mile to the west is Walcot Park. The large red-brick house at Walcot was built for Clive of India. A grove of trees was planted to spell out the word Plassey, the scene of Clive's famous victory in 1757. The trees were felled in the Second World War, as it was feared they would be an easy landmark for German bombers.

Make your way to a stile at the opposite end of the settlement to the point at which you entered. Cross the stile and follow a grassy track to your right through the pines. The path leads gently downhill and comes to a junction with another track. Go left. The path leads down through the forest of pine, oak and beech. Through the trees to your left, the dark pools of water are intermittently illuminated by a shaft of sunlight. Continue descending until you meet the broad forestry track leading around Sunnyhill.

Go left down the track. Keep to the track heading downhill, ignoring a track veering right. The route leads down through the pines to a farm gate, with a small pool on the left. Go through the gate and continue straight on along an uneven lane. Pass a house on your left and walk through the village of Guilden Down. There are superb views looking down to Clun and the Clun Forest beyond. Along the high ridge of the forest runs Offa's Dyke, the former defensive border with Wales.

The lane leads you down past the youth hostel on your left. As you come into Clun follow the road round to your right. Go left into Ford Street, and left again into High Street. The Sun Inn is on your right.

Bishop's Castle
The Three Tuns

Standing at the top of the town, the Three Tuns is a fount of good cheer, its high spirits spilling into the steep High Street of Bishop's Castle. It all begins in the red-brick tower, which makes this one of the most historic home-brew pubs in the country. The beers descend the tower, floor by floor, following the brewing process, until they arrive in the pub as XXX Bitter, Light Mild and strong seasonal brews, such as Old Scrooge.

While the brewery is Victorian, the pub itself is 17th century and has held a full licence since 1642. The décor is simple, with cream walls, dark beams, sturdy oak furniture and an assemblage of antique farming implements and enamel signs. The clientele is a rich mixture, with a strong local flavour.

The bar menu includes a wide variety of home-cooked dishes: steaks, pies, and vegetarian, as well as an excellent range of British puddings and snacks such as soup, filled rolls and baked potatoes. There is a bar, lounge bar, conservatory, terrace and beer garden. Children are welcome.

Opening hours are 11.30 am to 3 pm, 6.30 pm to 11 pm, and on Fridays, Saturdays and bank holidays till 5 pm in the afternoon. Tours of the Grade I listed building can be arranged.

Telephone: 0588 638797.

How to get there: Bishop's Castle is off the A488 from Shrewsbury. There is a regular bus service from Shrewsbury, Ludlow and Knighton.

Parking: There is limited parking outside the pub. Alternatively, use the public car park in Station Road.

Length of the walk: 4 miles. Map: OS Landranger 137 Ludlow, Wenlock Edge and surrounding area (GR 323890).

Some of Shropshire's most dramatic views surround the hillside on which Bishop's Castle is built: the Long Mynd to the east; the Stiperstones to the north; Bury Ditches to the south; Clun Forest and the Welsh hills to the west. This walk takes you across the more gentle hills around the town, through a valley graced with ancient oaks and the tangled meanderings of a golden stream, and finally a spectacular descent offers views of the town from the castle at the top to the church at its foot.

The Walk
Go left from the pub, up Salop Street. At the end of the street on your right is the seating area where the market house once stood. In the wall is the coat of arms of the Earl of Powis. The elephant is a reminder of Clive of India and the days when this charming town was 'the rottenest borough' in England. The smallest borough in the country, it nevertheless returned two MPs to Parliament. Clive, who wanted to match his immense fortune with corresponding political power, 'bought' Bishop's Castle's two seats when he acquired the Walcot estate. Until the Second World War a grove of trees spelled out the word Plassey, scene of his famous victory in 1757. For fear of acting as a landmark for German bombers, the trees were felled. Walcot is on the B4385, from Bishop's Castle to Lydbury North. The house and park are open to the public each August bank holiday, for a traction engine rally.

Turn left down Market Square. Cattle, driven along the Kerry Ridgeway from Wales, used to be sold here. On your left down the twisting cobbled way is the 'House on Crutches', so called because of the timber posts supporting the weighty 17th century gable.

Continue along Welsh Street. This is part of the Kerry Ridgeway. Said to be the oldest road in Wales, it dates back to the early Bronze Age, when it was used to carry the trade of axe heads and flint tools. It became the great drove road for cattle farmers from North Wales. The castle was situated on the parkland up to your right. Founded in the early 12th century by the Bishops of Hereford, the castle predates the town, which was laid out in a rectangular grid on the slope below. The castle was destroyed during the Civil War, and now all that

101

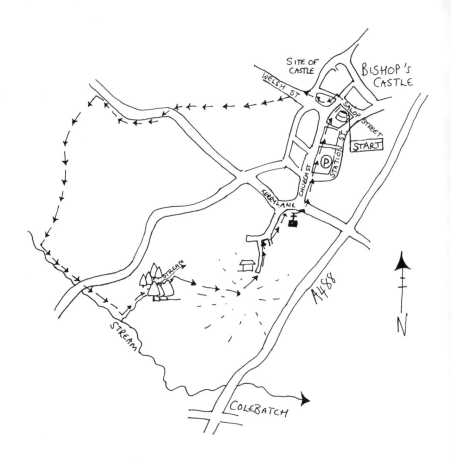

remains is a small section of the wall.

On your left, just past the terrace of cottages, where the turnpike gate once stood, is a kissing-gate leading into a field. Cross the field diagonally. The stile is about three-quarters of the way down the right-hand boundary. Cross the second field to a stile on the opposite boundary to the right of the gateway. In the third field, walk diagonally uphill, through the line of trees running down the centre of the field, and up to a stile in the top left-hand corner. Go over the stile and on to the lane.

Go right up the lane. Halfway up the hill a footpath is marked in the hedgerow on your left. Cross the stile and the field to a waymarked gate on the opposite boundary. Cross the next field diagonally to a metal farm gate in the far left-hand corner. Cross this gate and then a

102

second farm gate immediately on your right, cutting the corner of the field.

This next very large field tumbles down into the valley. Walk straight down, until you reach the footpath following the course of the stream. Go left and continue to follow the stream until the path emerges on a muddy lane.

Cross straight over the lane to the gate opposite, and continue following the stream. Continue as the stream meanders in tangled twists and turns, until you see a mixed woodland up on the hillside on your left.

Walk to the end of the field running beneath the wood. At the boundary fence, if not too dry, there should be a tributary stream flowing down from the wood. Do not cross the stream, but follow it up to the left, over a stile, and into the wood. Keep the stream on your right until you meet a footbridge. Cross the bridge. The path leads away from the stream slightly, and then through a gate and into a field.

Go through the gate immediately on your left. This field is shaped rather like a huge pair of trousers, with a triangular kink in the opposite boundary fence. Head diagonally across the field to the tip of the triangle (the crotch). Keeping the triangle on your left, walk up the boundary (the inside leg), until you cross a stile.

Keeping the boundary on your left, cross several fields, heading down toward a white house. Go down the track beside the white house as it veers round to the left, through a gate and comes out on Church Lane.

Follow the high red-brick wall round to the left, noticing the stream running down the street. St John Baptist's, built in 1291, was almost destroyed in the Civil War. That the tower survived testifies to its squat, Norman solidity.

Turn right up Kerry Lane and take the first left up Church Street. See how the short streets cross the main street at right angles, typical of a 'plantation' town. Even today the town has hardly expanded beyond this medieval blueprint.

Pass the 17th century Boars Head Inn and continue as Church Street merges into High Street. At the top of High Street, on the right, is the town hall, built around 1760. The stocks and whipping post once stood in front of it. In the 18th century theft, however, minor, would be punished with a public whipping, while an offender who had been drunk, would spend a short spell in the stocks. Keeping this sobering thought in mind, continue up Market Square and retrace your steps to the Three Tuns.

25 Hopesgate
The Stables Inn

It is not by chance that this 17th century pub lies off the beaten track. The drovers coming from Wales would take this route to avoid the tolls on the main route through the Hope Valley. Today people are drawn to the Stables for the homely atmosphere, the friendly welcome, and above all for the food.

The food is home cooked and almost entirely of local produce. Starters can include potted shrimps, a selection of local sausages, or baked mushrooms with melted Brie. You can tuck into a hearty main course of country rabbit and cider casserole with dumplings, half a locally smoked chicken with apples, apricot and cider, creamy fish pie or a cheese, tomato and aubergine bake. There is an impressive array of home-cooked puddings: apple crumble, Norwegian cream, bread-and-butter pudding, or local farmhouse ice-creams. There is a local real ale, Wood Special, as well as Double Dragon, Tetley and a guest beer.

The bar has an open stone fireplace, antique oak tables and wheel-back chairs. From the beams hangs a collection of ceramic jugs and loving cups. Install yourself in the cosy dining-room or on the front terrace overlooking Long Mountain. Children are welcome in the eating area.

Opening hours are 11.30 am to 2.30 pm, 7 pm to 11 pm and 12 noon to 2 pm, 7 pm to 11 pm in winter. The pub is closed on Mondays. Meals and snacks are served 12 noon to 1.30 pm Tuesday to Sunday, 7 pm to 8.30 pm Wednesday, Thursday, Friday and Saturday evenings (booking is advisable). Telephone: 0743 891344.

How to get there: The Stables Inn is signposted off the A488, Shrewsbury to Bishop's Castle road. The turning is a short distance from the village of Hope as you head to Bishop's Castle.

Parking: There is a large car park opposite the pub.

Length of the walk: 3½ miles. Map: OS Landranger 126 Shrewsbury and surrounding area (GR 342019).

This is a short walk, over easy-going terrain, offering superb views throughout. The outward journey takes you over fields and along well-made tracks before making a short ascent to Bromlow Callow. This hill, crowned with Scots pines, is a much-loved Shropshire landmark. It figures in 'Gone to Earth', Mary Webb's novel, and is thought locally to be a favourite haunt of Shropshire witches. From the summit you can see far into Wales and over the surrounding hills. The return journey takes you over Luckley Hill, across the fields to the Stables Inn.

The Walk
Leave the car park and go right down the lane for a few yards to a waymarked stile on your right. The stile leads into a large ploughed field. Walk diagonally across the field. The gateway is just left of the far left-hand corner of the field. Cross a tiny turfed-over bridge immediately in front of the gate. Go through the gate into a small field. Cross the field to a gateway directly opposite. Go through the gateway and cross the third field to a rough stile to the left of the houses. Go over the stile and cross the short field to a gateway in the holly hedge opposite. Go left through another gate to a metalled lane.

Go right along the lane to the T-junction. Turn left climbing uphill until the lane forks. Bear right following the sign to Pentirvin. The lane heads downhill to the cluster of stone buildings at Pentirvin. Continue straight on. The lane becomes a muddy track leading uphill. Follow the track until it deposits you on the lane with Bromlow Callow directly ahead.

Cross the lane and go over the stile opposite, to make the short ascent to Bromlow Callow. Walk straight uphill to the clump of Scots pines and European larch. Notice the drystone walls on the hillside. Go over the stile into the copse.

105

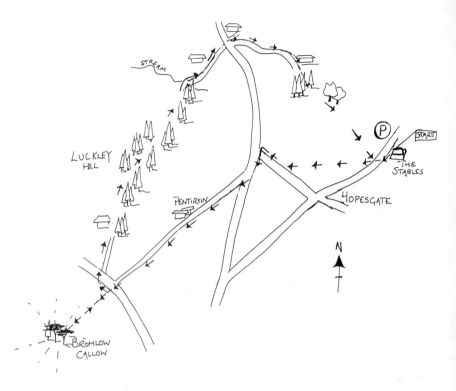

Callow comes from the Old English word for bald. The trees crowning the hill are all that remains of a much larger plantation established in Victorian times. Early this century the plantation was reduced to form this striking landmark. The Callow stands 800 ft above sea-level. The dramatic location of these lonely pines has given rise to 20th century myths. Rumours abound of the witches on Bromlow Callow.

To preserve this extraordinary copse the County Council enlisted the help of the Royal Forestry Society. In 1982 it adopted the copse to commemorate its centenary, fencing it off from livestock and replanting the larch and Scots pines.

Retrace your steps downhill to the road. To your far right you can see the white spoil heaps of Snailbeach lead mine, once thought to be the richest lead mine in Europe. Hope Valley was also mined for lead. Hope Brook had exposed the veins, making mining particularly easy. The mines were worked constantly from the mid 18th century. The mine was known as Roman Gravels because it was thought to be the principal site of the Roman lead mines. Oak spades and pigs of lead bearing the stamp of the Roman Emperor Hadrian were found in the

106

adit, proving that the mine had been exploited in the early second century. One of these pigs is now on display in the British Museum. In 1890 the mine still employed 200 men, 50 more than the Snailbeach mine. It finally closed down in 1900.

On the road go left and then go right down a track to Luckley Gate. Follow the track as it dips and then rises up to a gate situated at the left-hand corner of a pine wood. Go through the gate. Keep to the right-hand side of this very large field as it climbs over Luckley Hill. The gate is on the opposite boundary near the far right-hand corner. Go through the gate and head for the telegraph pole in the centre of the field, before dropping down to another gate in the far right-hand corner. Go through the gate and over a stream. Walk alongside the pine forest until you come to a waymarked gate on your right, leading into the pine wood. Go through the gate and follow the path downhill out of the wood. Keep in a straight line, walking across the short expanse of grass toward the corner of the pine wood. Round to your right is a track crossing a stream. Follow the track. It leads uphill, past some farm buildings and on to a lane. If you look back you can see Bromlow Callow on the horizon.

Opposite are two farm tracks. Take the right-hand track, crossing a cattle grid and curving around the hill on your right. The track ends at a group of red-brick dwellings. Continue straight on, to a stile with three waymarkers nailed to it. Cross the stile and head diagonally right, heading for the boulders lying in the field. You will see the stile ahead of you, leading into another pine forest. Cross the stile. Follow the path left, past a pheasantry, and over a further stile into a field.

The field climbs steeply uphill and has a line of trees running down the centre. The gateway is at the top of the field, just to the right of the line of trees. Go through the gate and keep to the right-hand boundary, heading over the summit of the hill. You can see the black ridge of the Stiperstones ahead of you. Go through the gate in the far right-hand corner of the field. Keep to the left-hand boundary of this last field to return to your starting point.

㉖ Crewgreen
The Fir Tree Inn

To Welsh drovers, a fir tree signaled a place where both they and their sheep or cattle could spend the night. For the drovers, coming down from the Welsh hills, the Fir Tree was their last night on home territory, before they stepped across the border into England. Today, the 17th century bar caters for another type of traveller: the holidaymaker heading into Wales.

The bar is traditional with an open fire. The bar food is all home-cooked including beef goulash, pork rib chops, lasagne, steaks and vegetarian meals. In the evenings you can dine in the newly opened Wishing Well Restaurant.

Graham and Betty Ingram, the licensees, discovered a well when they were building a wall in the car park and decided to build a restaurant around it. The restaurant is entirely built of old stone, and the well, whose water was once used to brew beer, now forms the centre-piece.

There are Banks's cask ales and draught cider. Opening hours are Monday to Sunday 11.30 am to 2.30 pm, 7 pm to 11 pm. The restaurant is open Monday to Sunday 12 noon to 2 pm, 7 pm to 9.45 pm (last orders).

Telephone: 0743 884243.

How to get there: The B4393 to Crewgreen is off the A458 Shrewsbury to Welshpool road or the A483 between Welshpool and Oswestry.

Parking: There is a car park outside the pub.

Length of the walk: 3½ miles. Map: OS Landranger 126 Shrewsbury and surrounding area (GR 326152).

Following the line of the Argae, an 18th century dyke, built by the world experts in flood control, the Dutch, the walk takes you to Melverley church, 'an architectural gem of truly national importance'. The tiny half-timbered church is perched on the bank of the river Vyrnwy, the regular vertical timbers contrasting beautifully with its natural setting. The return journey cuts across the fields, back to the dyke, and then follows the course of the Severn. It is a gentle walk on the flat and should suit even the least energetic of pilgrims.

The Walk
From the pub cross the road. Walk slightly to the right and over the stile into the field. Walk down the left-hand side of the field towards the bridge. The stile is in the bottom left-hand corner of the field. Cross the stile into a coppice. Walk up through the coppice and cross a second stile to the road.

Turn right and go over the bridge. All the water draining down from the Welsh mountains flows under this bridge. The hill behind you is Breidden Hill, crowned by Rodney's Column. On your left you can see the meeting of the Severn and the Vyrnwy. The three isolated Scots pines were a signal to drovers coming down from the Welsh hills. The pines (in England the same message is carried by yews) indicated that there was accommodation for them and their animals. Tragically, the Cymerau Inn, which stood at the confluence of the rivers, was hit by a terrible flood. The family tried to reach safety at Crewgreen, but were drowned.

Immediately after the bridge, go through the arch of hawthorn and ash and over the stile to the river bank. You can see the flood-water gauges next to the bridge. In gentle currents swans glide on the river and cows graze in the shallow waters.

Walk between the river and the boundary toward the green sluice gates, then head for the ridge of earth to the left of the corner of the boundary fence. Follow the ridge through the gate. This ridge of earth is a dyke, known as the Argae. It was built by a party of Dutch engineers in 1790. Prior to the dyke, even the village of Crewgreen was subject to terrible flooding.

Cross the field toward the grey farm buildings. Enter the farmyard at the right-hand corner of the field. Follow the farm track through a

109

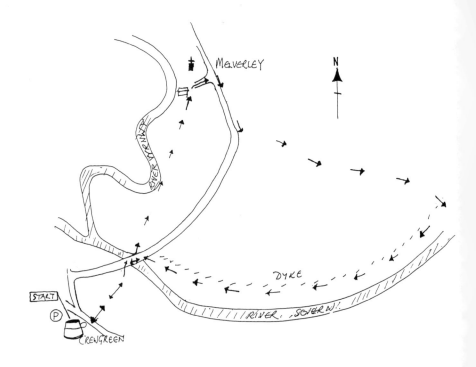

gate. On your left peeking through the trees is Melverley church. Continue straight ahead onto the lane.

On the church gate is written 'Most Motivated Village 1991'. Erosion of the river bank was undermining the structure of the church and the village raised £250,000 to carry out a major programme of stabilisation.

The building has stood here for 400 years, replacing a Saxon church which was destroyed by fire. It is built of vertical oak timbers with rendered lath and plaster infill, and is one of only two remaining timber-framed churches in the county. The simplicity of this tiny black and white church represents religion on a very peaceful, human scale.

The interior has a similar simplicity. The first thing that strikes you is the smell of wood. It is pegged throughout, with 18th century oak settles, a Jacobean altar that looks like a small oak table, and a font which has been here for over 1,000 years. The gallery is one enormous piece of oak. When it was lowered into place it got wedged at an angle, and it has not moved since.

In times of national crisis, the monarch would command a special service to be held. Between 1739 and 1900 35 special services were held at Melverley. They included services for the Jacobite rebellion, the 1756 earthquake, the Sikh rebellion in India, Queen Victoria's safe delivery in childbirth, the Crimean War, crop failure, the Indian Mutiny and the Boer War.

Leaving the church go straight on down the lane. On your right is the Tontine pub. A tontine is a kind of financial Russian roulette. Each member of the tontine would put in an initial sum of money, and annually received a small sum in interest. As the initial investors died, so the annual sum increased, until the last surviving member received the whole sum. This particular tontine was established by the Severn boatmen.

Go right at the pub. Walk down the lane to where the road forks. Cross the gate on your left. Walk straight across the field to a stile next to the ash tree in the opposite boundary. Follow the right-hand boundary and cross a stile in the right-hand corner. Walk diagonally across the next field to a gateway in the top left-hand corner. Go through the gate and on to a crossroads of two farm tracks.

At the meeting of the two farm tracks go through the farm gateway diagonally opposite. Walk diagonally across the field. The stile is just to the left of a kink in the opposite field boundary. Walk straight across the next field toward the point where the right-hand hedge ends. Continue in the same direction until you reach the dyke. Follow the dyke around to your right. The Argae was repaired by Thomas Telford. This section remains remarkably intact.

Continue to follow the Argae alongside the Severn, walking toward the bridge. The bridge once carried the railway over the river and is of a utilitarian, almost military design. Cross numerous stiles on the dyke, until you reach the field next to the bridge. Walk diagonally across this field, towards the river bank. The stile is immediately on the right-hand side of the bridge. Cross the stile and walk up to the road. Go left, back over the bridge. Hop over the stiles on the left-hand side. Retrace your steps across the field to the Fir Tree Inn.

㉗ Queen's Head
The Queen's Head

Built at the height of 'canal mania', this grand Georgian pub conveys the spirit of optimism out of which it was born. Standing high on the canal bank above Aston Locks, from the late 18th century until the 1930s it slaked the thirst of the boatmen passing through this small rural community.

On February 6th 1936 the canal burst just north of Queen's Head, it was dammed off and is now 4 miles of peaty bog. But the Queen's Head still towers up on the canal bank, a landmark for miles around.

This popular family pub offers a large menu as well as snacks such as jacket potatoes. Starters include chicken liver and brandy pâté, and mushroom, leeks and smoked bacon topped with a cheese sauce. Main courses might be sautéed chicken with broccoli and prawns, or halibut with tiger prawns and garlic butter. Tempting home-made puddings such as walnut fudge cake and banoffi pie complete the picture. There is a beer garden and picnic tables on the terrace. Theakston Old Peculier and Dry Blackthorn cider are on draught. Children are welcome. Opening hours are Monday to Sunday 12 noon to 2.30 pm, 6 pm to 11 pm (10 pm Sunday). Food is served 12 noon to 2.30 pm, 6 pm to 10 pm.

Telephone: 0691 610255.

How to get there: the village of Queen's Head is just off the A5, 5 miles south of Oswestry.

Parking: There is a large car park at the Queen's Head.

Length of the walk: 5 miles. Map: OS Landranger 126 Shrewsbury and surrounding area (GR 338268).

For centuries the faithful made this pilgrimage to Winifred's Well. The healing waters bubble up from beneath a tiny black and white cottage, making this one of the most charming holy wells in the country. The walk takes you across Oswestry Golf Course and over fields to the hidden well. It returns via the Montgomery Canal. This section of the canal, long since abandoned by narrow boats, has been reclaimed by the birds, plants and animals.

The Walk
Turn right out of the Queen's Head and walk up the road to the A5. Turn right on the A5 and cross the road and turn left into the entrance to Oswestry Golf Club.

Cross the car park, heading toward the clubhouse. Walk over the paved area in front of the clubhouse to the line of fir trees. Go left, walking between the line of fir trees and the 8th tee. Continue walking in a straight line through a grove of large oaks. Then walk downhill to the left, through some silver birches, past a sign on your right, 'Practice Ground, Replace Divots'. Continue in a straight line past the 9th tee and 8th green to a section of rough and woodland to the back of the 17th tee. On the other side of the fairway, to your right, is a deeply sunken, grassy track running over the crest of the hill. Cross the fairway carefully and walk down the sunken track. The track runs behind the 13th tee and continues in a straight line down to a footbridge.

Cross the bridge into a short field. Walk directly across the field to a stile opposite. Go over the stile. Ignore the broad track to your left and continue in a straight line, following a wire fence. Go past a pond on your right and up to a stile. Cross the stile into a very large field. Walk round the edge of the field, heading towards a white house in the far left-hand corner. Go through the farm gate on the left-hand boundary fence, just before the far left-hand corner of the field.

Go straight ahead along the farm track. Keep left where the track forks. Straight ahead of you is a stile beside a gateway. Cross the stile and walk through an avenue of oak, chestnut and ash. Continue in a straight line past Fox Hall Farm to your left, keeping to the left-hand boundary. Just past the farm is a stile in the left-hand hedgerow leading to a track. Cross the stile and turn right down the track.

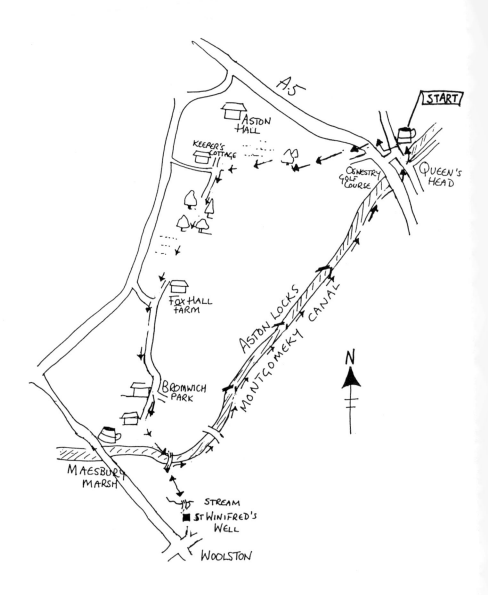

Where the track meets a lane continue straight on. Follow the lane, ignoring a waymarked stile on the right, as it twists round to the gates of Bromwich Park. Go through the gate to Bromwich Park, a large house with stables and an elaborate façade. Continue straight on past the house through the farm gate opposite.

Follow the muddy track until you come to a stone cottage. Do not go down the track to the cottage. Cross the stile on the left. Follow the fence straight ahead down the right-hand side of the field. Where the fence bends right at a right angle, go right also. There is a path heading upward to a footbridge over the Montgomery Canal.

Go over the bridge and down to your right on to the towpath. Cross the stile into the field to make the short pilgrimage to St Winifred's Well. Follow a ridge of earth diagonally across the field to the far left-hand corner. Go over a stile and follow the hedgerow to your right.

The hedgerow leads to a footbridge crossed by two stiles. Go over the bridge to the pool of water running from the tiny black and white building. This is St Winifred's Well. Below the porch you can see the spring emerging from beneath the sandstone plinth. At Holywell in Clwyd, St Winifred had spurned the amorous advances of a prince. In his anger he cut off her head, and a spring gushed forth on the spot. In the reign of Stephen, St Winifred's body was brought from Holywell to Holy Cross in Shrewsbury. On the journey the body was laid to rest here at Woolston. Another spring surged from the ground. The holy well became a place of pilgrimage.

Return to the canal bridge across the fields. Cross the stile onto the towpath. If you make a ½ mile detour to your left along the towpath you reach the wharf at Maesbury Marsh. This was the nearest wharf to Oswestry. Goods would be transported from the canal to the town by horse-drawn wagons. The wharf is one of the best-preserved along the canal, with disused lime-kilns and an Agent's House with a large bay-window in the style of Thomas Telford.

Turn right along the towpath. Go through the bridge to Aston Locks. The locks are undergoing restoration. Voluntary work by the Shropshire Union Canal Society began on the Montgomery Canal in 1968. In 1987 an Act of Parliament was passed to reopen the canal. Volunteers from the Waterway Recovery Group have restored the flight of locks at Frankton and are still working on the locks here at Aston.

During the decades in which the canal has been free from human activity, wildlife has taken up residence. The banks are a habitat for foxes, badgers, water voles and shrews. Water birds include swans, moorhens, mallards, coots and herons. The yellow flag iris, yellow water lily, bur-reed and rare and common pond weeds are a small selection of the flora to be spotted on the waterway. Follow the canal towpath through Aston Locks. When you reach the modern road bridge passing over the canal follow the path under the bridge. Climb up to the road opposite the Queen's Head.

28 Priest Weston
The Miner's Arms

As I rolled down the 1 in 5 drop to Priest Weston I heard the strains of flutes and bagpipes. Children and dogs were playing in the beer garden and dancing with the adults, in the lane, beside the hollyhocks and hanging baskets. The Miner's Arms is the perfect venue for an annual folk festival: revelry has been a ritual in this area since the Druids discovered a holy well nearby.

During the heyday of the barytes mine there were two pubs in Priest Weston – the other one was for the bosses. The Miner's Arms has retained its down-to-earth character. The décor is genuine: next to the large open fire there is an anvil from the days when this was both pub and blacksmith's shop; old photographs and letters catalogue the history of the Weston barytes mine. They offer 'low key' and low-price bar food: a beef stew, a bowl of soup or a pasty (in true miner's style) must be the ideal accompaniment to a walk across the awe-inspiring hillsides of this corner of Shropshire. There are also ploughman's and salads. Welsh Brewers, Bass, Worthington Best Bitter and cider are all on draught.

The landlord, a helpful and jovial enthusiast, can organise food for large walking parties and accommodation in the village (bed and

breakfast or camping). Opening hours are 11 am to 4 pm, 6 pm to 11 pm.
Telephone: 093 872 352.

How to get there: Priest Weston lies 17 miles south-west of Shrewsbury, off the A488, Shrewsbury to Bishop's Castle road.

Parking: There is a car park behind the pub.

Length of the walk: 4 miles or 5 miles with a detour up Corndon Hill. Map: OS Landranger 137 Ludlow, Wenlock Edge and surrounding area (GR 291973).

Mitchell's Fold, Shropshire's most celebrated stone circle, continues to fascinate and mystify visitors. While its purpose remains uncertain, the ring and the numerous prehistoric relics that surround it have become the focus for myth and ancient ritual. The walk takes you via quiet country lanes and well-worn tracks to the top of Stapley Hill, along the ancient cultivation ridges, to the stone circle. The locality is equally rich in industrial archaeology. Exploited since Roman times for its lead, in the 19th and early 20th centuries the hills were mined for the bright white mineral, barytes. The route passes abandoned mine shafts, and overgrown spoil heaps, following the line of the old railway track to the foot of Corndon Hill. Here you can either take a short detour to the summit, or return directly down the hillside and into the Miner's Arms. Throughout the walk there are beautiful views of the surrounding hillsides including the Welsh mountains, the Stiperstones, Corndon and Lan Fawr.

The Walk

Leaving the car park, turn right into Priest Weston. At the grassy triangle in the road continue uphill past the village hall and an interesting piece of corrugated-iron architecture. Continue down the high-hedged lane for about 1½ miles, passing Weston Farm, until you come to a lane on your right, signposted 'Mitchell's Fold'.

The lane climbs steeply, passing a sheered rock-face on the left, before arriving at a white-painted stone house and a gateway across the lane. Go through the gate and continue up the lane. Keep an eye out for lapwings and curlews gliding over the moorland, and the yellow mountain pansy which flowers on the hillside in summer.

Where the lane veers sharply right, take the grassy track leading straight through the bracken, up to the summit. When you arrive at the top, go right. follow the grassy ridges running along the summit, until you reach the stone circle.

This circle of stones dates from around 2000–1400 BC. Originally there were probably 30 stones, but only 14 remain. Like all standing stones, their precise purpose remains a mystery, but the theories

117

abound. The highland location is typical. The panoramic views of the surrounding hillsides and the exposure to the open sky lends weight to the theory that stone circles are linked to the worship of nature. In the Hoarstone stone circle, at the Northern end of Stapeley Hill, there are gaps which align with Bromlow Callow, the Stiperstones and Corndon Hill. Such alignments with landmarks, or with astronomical movements, have led some to attribute a scientific function to the circles. Mitchell's Fold, however, may have played the more prosaic role as a 'market place' for Lan Fawr Bronze Age axe factory. The axe factory was discovered below Corndon Hill. It lies on the Kerry Ridgeway, the great drovers' road bordering England and Wales. The Ridgeway dates back to about 2000 BC, when it carried the trade of axe heads and flint tools. Axe heads manufactured at Lan Fawr have been found as far away as Cornwall.

Continue along the ridge top, past the site of the Druid castle, known as the Whetstones, toward the elegant, heather-clad lines of Corndon Hill, and her tufty, nobbly sister, Lan Fawr. The almost circular cone of Corndon is formed of a sill of dolerite piercing the softer shale of the surrounding hillsides.

When you reach the road continue straight ahead. The patchy growth on the field to your left roughly disguises the spoil heaps of the Weston barytes mine, in operation at least until the 1930s. If you look at the stones in the spoil heaps next to the road you will find a bright, white, quartz-like stone. Barytes, also known as 'heavy spar', is the principal ore of barium, and often occurs in areas rich in lead. It was used to produce the paint pigment permanent white, or to give weight to certain papers and fabrics.

Where the road veers sharply left, continue straight ahead along a bridleway, formerly the railway track leading to the mines. In the field on your right the fences enclose the abandoned mine shafts.

Continue along the track until you reach the base of Corndon Hill, where the track veers to your right. If you wish to take the short but energetic detour up Corndon Hill, cross the old stile on your left, at the beginning of the conifer woodland. On the summit (about ½ mile) is a cairn, a Bronze Age burial mound constructed of stone. Otherwise continue to follow the track right until you reach a waymarked path, next to a field boundary on your right. At first the descending path is not easy to locate, but if you walk diagonally across the field you will meet the path wheeling down through the bracken. Cross the stile next to a hawthorn bush. The steep descent reveals spectacular views before emerging at the meeting of two tracks.

Ignore the track to your left and go straight on down the track opposite. Follow the lane past the cottages until it deposits you on the road opposite the Miner's Arms.

118

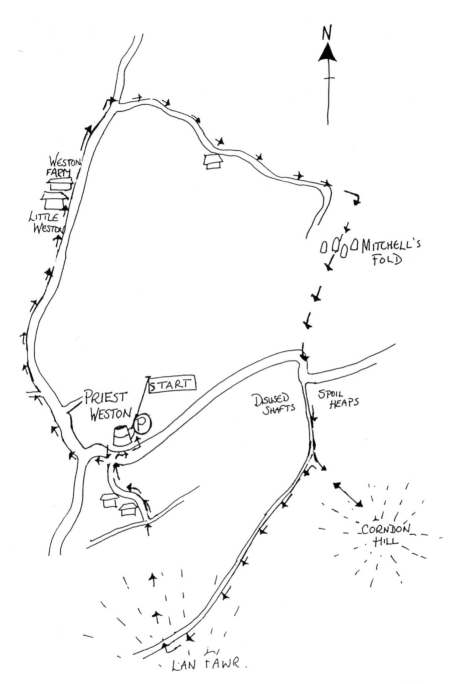

N

WESTON FARM

LITTLE WESTON

MITCHELL'S FOLD

PRIEST WESTON

START

P

DISUSED SHAFTS

SPOIL HEAPS

CORNDON HILL

LAN FAWR.

29 Oswestry
The Fox Inn

You enter this tiny timber pub through a cleft oak door on the side, to be greeted by an open fire and nobbly oak beams decorated with horse brasses. The only major change to the pub since the 17th century appears to be the loss of the gable. The ill-fated gable was very low and projected over the pavement. One day Richard Smale was making his way from the Wynnstay Hotel to the centre of town, sporting his silk top hat. Unfortunately the hat was struck by the gable. Rather than resolving in future to remove his hat, Mr Smale removed the offending gable.

The Fox Inn serves classic home-cooked pub food and snacks: pies omelettes, jacket potatoes, steak, plaice and chips and toasted sandwiches. Real ales are Marston's Bitter, Pedigree Bitter, Banks's Mild and a guest beer. Opening hours are 11 am to 3 pm, 7 pm to 11 pm. Food is served 11 am to 2.30 pm, 7 pm to 9 pm.

Telephone: 0691 679669.

How to get there: The Fox Inn is in Church Street in the centre of Oswestry.

Parking: There is no car park at the pub, but Oswestry has several pay and display car parks in the centre of town.

Length of the walk: 3 miles. Map: OS Landranger 126 Shrewsbury and surrounding area (GR 295285).

It is fitting that Oswestry should be the birthplace of Britain's most distinguished war poet, Wilfred Owen. Lying between Offa's Dyke and Wat's Dyke, its turbulent history includes the death of a king, marks of Civil War shelling and one of the finest Iron Age hill forts in Europe. Oswestry is more than a much fought-over border town: the hill fort is said to be the birthplace of Queen Guinevere and where the bard from King Arthur's court composed the oldest surviving Celtic verse in the country. The Wednesday street market, the largest in Shropshire and the Borders, rings with Welsh and English voices. The walk takes you to the site of Prince Madoc's castle, the Owen Memorial, through the four gateways which once punctuated the town walls, and up to the hill fort. You return to the town centre following the line of Wat's Dyke, along the disused railway track.

The Walk

Starting at The Fox Inn, turn left. The pillar on this side of the street marks the site of New Gate. This is the first of four gates allowing access through the town walls. The walls were built in the 13th century and were over a mile long.

Continue down Church Street to the traffic lights. In the 1950s, the house on the left-hand corner belonged to Frank Bough, of *Grandstand*, *Nationwide* and breakfast TV fame. Go right down Upper Brook Street. Take the first right up a cobbled alley-way and through a lych-gate known as the Griddle Gate.

In 1407 a grammar school was founded in the timber and brick building on your left. It was one of the earliest secular schools in Britain. The lower floor is now a tearoom and tourist information centre. Upstairs is a small town museum, containing a charming collection of enamel signs. It is worth a visit, if only to see the eccentric tilt of the wooden floor.

Both the church and the town take their name from Oswald, the Christian king of Northumbria. He was slain at the Battle of Oswestry by the pagan ruler of Mercia, Penda. The 12th century church tower acted as a key observation point in the Civil War. The hole above the vestry door is said to have been made by a Roundhead cannon-ball. Inside is a monument to Hugh Yale whose family founded Yale University.

Bear to the left through the avenue of yews. Go through the gate in the top left-hand corner of the churchyard. Turn right down a tree-lined way known as Broadwalk. Just before you re-emerge on Church

121

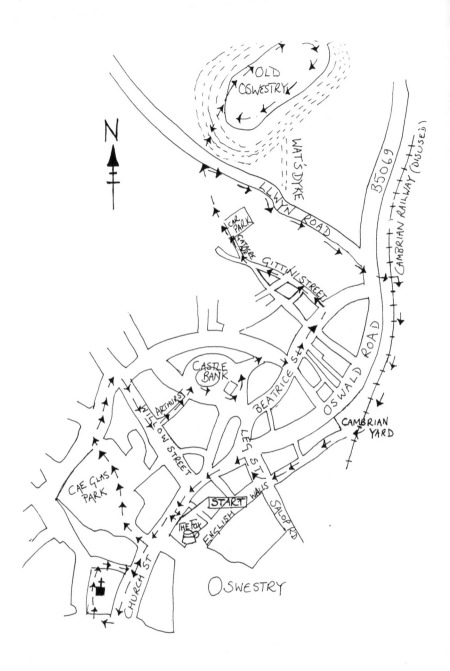

OLD OSWESTRY

WAT'S DYKE

LLWYN ROAD

B5069

CAMBRIAN RAILWAY (DISUSED)

CAR PARK

CLADRE CRE

GITTIN STREET

CASTLE BANK

ARTHUR ST

WILLOW STREET

BEATRICE ST

OSWALD ROAD

CAMBRIAN YARD

LEG ST

CAE GLAS PARK

START

WALLS

ENGLISH

SALOP RD

THE FOX

CHURCH ST

OSWESTRY

Street, notice the plaque on the left-hand wall. Wilfred Owen was born in Oswestry. This sensitive tribute allows his poetry to speak for itself.

Back on the main road, turn left. Go left again through the gates to the war memorial. Often the young men from a community would serve in the same regiment, thus risking the loss of a whole generation. Oswestry suffered particularly heavy losses in both world wars.

Follow the path running to the right through Cae Glas Park. Leave the park by the gate in the top right-hand corner, emerging on Welsh Walls. Go right. Turn right again into Willow Street, where a plaque marks the site of the Willow or Walia Gate on the road to Wales.

The Butchers' Arms is one of the town's oldest inns. In 1672 it was granted a royal licence to allow the dissenting Independent Church of Sweeney to worship in one of the rooms. Turn left through the archway beside the Butchers' Arms, into Arthur Street. Continue up the narrow street to Castle Bank.

Castle Bank is the highest point in the town. The two pillars flanking the steps mark the position of Beatrice Gate. 'Toll Through' was carved into the stone. The words can still be deciphered on the left-hand gate post. Go through the gates and climb up on to Castle Mound to the remains of the castle walls. The view looks over the red-brick streets of Oswestry to the clearly defined ramparts of Old Oswestry Hill Fort.

The castle was built prior to the Norman Conquest by the Welsh Prince Madoc Ap Meredydd to control border trade. It changed hands frequently in the border wars. During the Civil War, Oswestry was a Royalist stronghold. The town was besieged by Parliamentarians and surrendered after the castle gate was mined. Cromwell ordered the castle to be destroyed.

Climb down from the mound back into the square. Take the second left, with the TSB building on your left, down Bailey Head. Turn left down Albion Hill and continue through the square, straight on, into Beatrice Street.

The gabled Fighting Cocks dates from the 14th century. Beatrice Gate stood outside the Plough Hotel. Continue, noticing how the street widens as soon as you leave the restrictions imposed by the town walls. Go left up Gittin Street. At the fork bear right to Gatacre Playing Fields.

Take the path running down the left of the car park, between a fence and a hawthorn hedge. Go through the kissing-gate into a field. Cross the field diagonally to a second kissing-gate leading to the lane.

Go through the gate opposite into the Hill Fort. The five concentric rings are known locally as Caer Ograu. It is said that Ograu's daughter, Guinevere, Arthur's bride, was born here. Llywarch Hen, Prince of

Cumbria and a bard in Arthur's court, came here to support Cynddylan of Powys against the Angles. The poems he wrote are the oldest surviving fragments of Celtic verse in Britain, and are available, in either English or Welsh, from Oswestry Library.

In the 8th century Wat's Dyke was built, incorporating the fort. To the north the straight line of the dyke can be seen following the hedgerows. It was probably built during the reign of Offa's predecessor, King Aethelbald, to mark the frontier of Mercia. Like Offa's Dyke it is a continuous bank of earth flanked by a west-facing ditch. It extends 38 miles, from north-west Shropshire to the estuary of the Dee. Oswestry, lying between the two dykes, was deemed neutral territory for trade between Danes, Saxons and Britons.

After leaving the fort, go left down the lane to the main road. Cross the road and go over the disused railway tracks via the old footbridge. Follow the path alongside the track toward the centre of town. At the green and white signal box the path recrosses the track. This was the headquarters of the Cambrian Railway. Wilfred Owen's father was stationmaster here. The Cambrian Railway Society now uses the yard to renovate steam engines, and runs a museum in one of the old engine sheds. As well as the steam trains, it has a collection of vintage bicycles, and railway and bicycle memorabilia.

Walk down the right-hand side of the car park to emerge opposite the cinema and the Black Gate, named after the last of the four gates. Turn right down Leg Street, left down Cross Street and back to The Fox Inn.

⓷⓪ Llanymynech
The Bradford Arms

Llanymynech straddles the Welsh border and has a history of mining dating back to the Romans. Amid this down-to-earth setting the Bradford Arms serves food lavish in every respect except price.

The red-brick frontage may appear slightly austere, but inside the bar combines elegance with warmth. The menu adds a touch of class to traditional dishes: the cheese platter includes cheeses such as Casel Blue, smoked Wedmore and Llanboidy, served with home-baked bread, celery and apple; lamb with creamy mint sauce or pork with parsnips appear regularly.

Round the side of the pub is an attractive patio, and the creeper-covered entrance to the restaurant. The restaurant offers specialities such as baked crab, beef forestière and venison. Opening hours are 12 noon to 2.30 pm (2 pm Sunday), 7 pm to 11 pm (10.30 pm Sunday). Bar food and restaurant 12 noon to 2 pm, 7 pm to 10 pm. Children are welcome.

Telephone: 0691 830582.

How to get there: Llanymynech is on the A483, 6 miles south of Oswestry. The pub is on the left-hand side of the main road. An hourly bus service runs between Oswestry, Llanymynech and Welshpool.

Parking: There is a car park behind the pub.

Length of the walk: 3 miles. Map: OS Landranger 126 Shrewsbury and surrounding area (GR 266210).

Where could you find a border town with more romance than Llanymynech, the only golf course in the world where you can drive off in one country and putt out in another, a pub where you can buy a drink from the bar in England but knock it back in Wales? The walk follows a reed-fringed canal backwater, which once bustled with limestone-laden boats, and climbs gently to the dramatic black cliffs of the limestone quarry, now a nature reserve. The heritage area, which concludes the walk, has one of the few surviving Hoffman kilns, a spectacular relic of the industrial past.

The Walk
Leave the car park and turn right down the main road. Immediately before the canal bridge go over the stile on your right and climb down to the towpath of the Montgomery Canal. Opened in 1796, the Ellesmere Canal, as it was then known, ran from Frankton to Llanymynech. It connected the limestone quarries to industry in the north-west of England. Limestone was essential as flux for the smelting of iron ore. Agriculture was also hungry for quicklime, an important fertiliser.

Contact with water causes quicklime to heat, eating through the bottom of narrow boats. It could, therefore, only be processed at its destination. The crude crushed limestone was transported and converted in one of over 100 kilns along the Ellesmere Canal. In its heyday, 45,000 tons of limestone and 11,000 tons of coal were transported each year along this waterway. Follow the towpath under the bridge. Walk along the canal until it reaches a dead-end at the road.

Cross a stile on to the road. Go right along the road for a few yards to a waymarked public footpath on your right. Follow the path up the left-hand side of the field. At the far end of the field it crosses a disused railway track. The Cambrian Railway was opened in 1860, connecting Llanymynech with Welshpool and Whitchurch. Now that quicklime could be transported overland without coming into contact with water, large limekilns were constructed below the quarries.

Keep to the left-hand side of the next field and go through the farm gate. This third field leads up to two stiles on the opposite boundary fence. Head for the stile on the right. From here the dramatic impact that the industry had on the landscape is apparent.

Cross the stile and walk down the next field to a stile in the bottom right-hand corner. The stile leads to a farm track. Go right down the farm track to the lane. On the lane go left climbing steeply uphill. Where the lane veers sharply left, take the right-hand fork. The lane

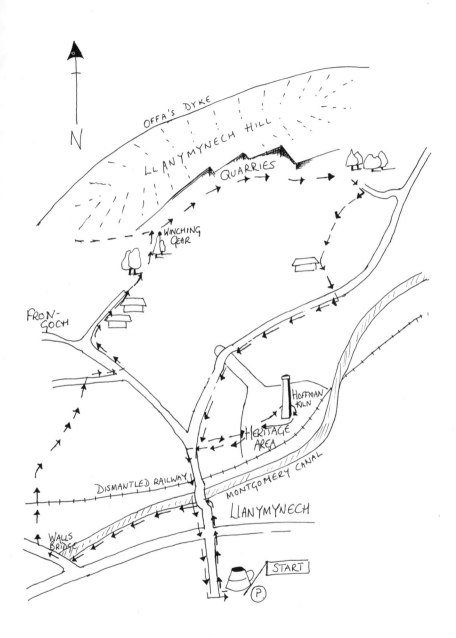

OFFA'S DYKE

LLANYMYNECH HILL

QUARRIES

WINCHING GEAR

FRON-GOCH

HOFFMAN KILN

HERITAGE AREA

DISMANTLED RAILWAY

MONTGOMERY CANAL

LLANYMYNECH

WALLS BRIDGE

START

P.

N

climbs steeply, passes several cottages and then comes to a dead-end. Go over the stile straight ahead of you. The path leads gently up through woodland on the south-eastern slope of the hill. It emerges at a red-brick ruin covered in ivy. This was a gin: wagons carrying limestone were attached to a beam by rope and lowered down the inclined plane. There the narrow boats would be loaded. Further down the incline is the entrance to a tunnel leading to another quarry.

To your left you will see a track following the contours of the hill. Go right along this track until you come face to face with the black cliffs of the quarry. The quarry's vastness gives us an idea of the scale of the limestone industry in this area. Less than 100 years ago it was still one of the busiest industries in the country. You can see how the stone has been cut back in a series of staggers, several small quarries eventually merging into this dramatic cavity.

Continue along the footpath as it brings you off the hill to a wooden gate leading out of the nature reserve. Go through the gate and then over the stile immediately on your right. Keep to the right-hand side of the first field. Go over the stile in the top right-hand corner and cross the second field diagonally to a gateway in the far left-hand corner. The path then leads left, down past an enticing walled garden. Cross the stile at the end of the path very carefully as it leads to a busy corner of the A483. Cross the road and go right toward Llanymynech. Cross a stone bridge and continue a short distance. The entrance to Llanymynech Heritage Area is on your left just before you reach the canal bridge. The stile is set back from the road. Cross the stile into the heritage area. There are waymarked routes around the various remains of the site. Make for the chimney to your left which towers over the heritage area. This was the flue of the revolutionary Hoffman Horizontal Ring Kiln.

This huge lozenge-shaped kiln, built in 1899, produced high-quality quicklime using very little coal. Inside, the kiln is supported by arched pillars of stone. The walls and ceiling are covered with white residue. It looks something like a cloister or an interior designed by the great Catalan architect, Gaudi. The kiln is made up of 14 chambers, each one accessed by an archway around the kiln. The first chamber would be filled with limestone and coal, ignited and sealed with bricks, then the second chamber was filled and sealed and the fire passed from the first chamber to the second and so on. Thus the kiln was in continuous operation. The kiln was only in production for 15 years, when competition from cheaper fertilisers caused it to close.

Follow one of the trail paths back to the road. Go left back over the canal bridge to the pub.